WHAT'S WRONG *With* MY HUSBAND?

*Your Lifeline for Standing for
Your Marriage and Surviving
Your Husband's Midlife Crisis*

AMY LAWRENCE

LAWRENCE, AMY, Author
WHAT'S WRONG WITH MY HUSBAND?
AMY LAWRENCE

Published by:
ELITE ONLINE PUBLISHING
63 East 11400 South
Suite #230
Sandy, UT 84070
EliteOnlinePublishing.com

ISBN: 979-8-9993587-4-5 (Paperback)
ISBN: 979-8-9993587-7-6 (eBook)
LCCN: 2025922428

FAM015000
FAM030000

www.standingspouses.com

Editing and publishing support provided by The Write Image Consulting, LLC and Write Your Life.

The contents of this book are for educational purposes and nothing contained herein should be construed as life or relationship advice. The information provided in this book are the opinions of the author and is not a complete analysis of every material fact for any situation. Some names and dates have been changed to protect privacy. Opinions expressed are subject to change without notice. Nothing contained herein is, in any way, a guarantee or assurance that following strategies outlined in this book will create success or security, and readers should understand that they are responsible for the actions they take or do not take as a result of reading this book. This book contains AI-assisted content.

This book contains references to common terms, phrases, and concepts that circulate widely in midlife crisis support communities, self-help literature, and coaching programs. All quoted material from published authors, speakers, or coaches is clearly attributed to its original source. The frameworks, methods, and stories presented here are original to the author, drawn from her personal experiences and coaching practice. Any resemblance to other works beyond cited material is purely coincidental.

Author Disclaimer to Reader
This book is based on my personal journey and my work coaching women whose husbands are in midlife crisis. I am not a therapist, counselor, or attorney, and this book is not meant to replace professional medical, mental health, or legal advice. What you will find here are stories, insights, and tools that have helped me and the women I have coached. Take what resonates, leave what does not, and always use your own wisdom in deciding what is right for you. If you need professional help, I encourage you to reach out to a qualified therapist, doctor, or attorney who can support your specific situation. Above all, know this: you are not alone, you are not powerless, and you can create a life you love — no matter what.

To every woman who thought her long-term marriage was rock solid—until one day, the foundation cracked beneath her feet and she suddenly found herself standing in the rubble of her husband's midlife crisis—this book is for you.

This is not just my story; it's a guide, a map, a flashlight for the dark, a lifeline.
May it help you feel seen, steady, and a little less alone.

PRAISES FOR AMY LAWRENCE AND *WHAT'S WRONG WITH MY HUSBAND?*

This book is like a warm hug for someone dealing with MLC. It's like a friend holding my hand, saying, "I see you. I know what you're going through. Let's get up. Here is how I handled it. Take my hand and I'll show you the way." A friend who is comforting me and laying the path and reassuring me that I will be ok. Giving me permission to be ok, or rather I *have to* be ok. Amy, your courage, strength, and determination feels like a win for all of us.

~ G.H.

I found Amy during the darkest chapter of my life, when the tears wouldn't stop and nothing made sense. I was drowning in a sea of confusion brought on by my partner's MLC, desperate for clarity. Amy doesn't just give answers; she offers something far more powerful: A way through the chaos. With compassion and full-hearted dedication, she guides on a journey of understanding and renewed focus. She helps rediscover how to heal, how to feel joy again, and how to move forward without ever feeling pressured to abandon hope. Amy is a true light when everything around feels impossibly dark. Thank you, Amy, for everything. I genuinely don't know where I'd be without you. And thankfully, I never have to find out.

~ Y.H.

Amy is so knowledgeable, caring, and empathetic. She has helped me to become a better, stronger version of myself. She is the calm in my life storm. I would not have gotten through this time as gracefully without her guidance.

~ S.

Amy gives great advice on how to navigate through not only your husband's crisis, but also through every other challenge life may throw at you. I found Amy and the information she provides to be more helpful and beneficial than the multiple therapists I had visited prior to finding Amy. She gives step-by-step guidance in a no-nonsense manner. Amy has a wealth of knowledge that she generously gives to those seeking guidance through a midlife crisis.

~ H.D.

Amy has been a beacon of light and hope during the darkest times of my life. She offers incredible warmth and empathy and helps you feel understood when no one in your life understands. More than that, she offers evidence-based tools to help change your mindset and get you off the bathroom floor and back on your feet to building your best life. No matter what happens with my husband, I know I will be ok thanks to her program.

~ E.R.

Take a Moment. Breathe.

The fact that you picked up this book means
you're searching for strength, clarity, and a way forward.

Download the Standing Spouses Starter Kit
to walk alongside you in this deeply personal season.

StandingSpouses.com/book

Includes videos and tools to support your next steps,
wherever you are in your journey.

With each video, you'll find a companion worksheet
to help you pause, capture your thoughts, and
apply what you're learning.

The workbook pairs with *What's Wrong With My Husband?*,
offering a way to reflect, process, and begin
healing in your life.

TABLE OF CONTENTS

FOREWORD

I am so excited about this book because I believe it is going to help so many people dealing with midlife crisis. I believe midlife crisis is on the rise. As we live longer, and societal norms evolve, the focus becomes more on our feelings and personal satisfaction. It's causing many of us to question our purpose and if we are happy. One could call this a midlife transition, but for some it becomes a true crisis and if you've had to deal with someone close going through this, it's mind boggling. A guide like this, laid out in such an easy-to-read format, sprinkled with wisdom Amy has gained through her own experience, is a true gem. There isn't another book like it. It's a starting point for those just entering the arena and drowning in their fears and confusion.

I met Amy on Facebook (of all things) in late 2020 or early 2021 while both of us were searching for answers to our husband's strange and crazy behavior. Amy and I connected on a support group for midlife crisis and quickly began private messaging and our friendship blossomed. Yes, we had this crisis in common, but we just really hit it off in all areas with enough interests between us that we weren't always talking about our husbands, our torment, our pain, our obsession etc. Sometimes we talked about fashion, or food, or travel, you know, other things.

We all hear midlife crisis and think of a red flashy sports car, a new tattoo or piercings, new clothes, younger friends etc. I'm not saying that those things don't happen, but what isn't discussed is the true crisis underneath. Thank goodness I had Amy to navigate this with. We bounced ideas off each other, encouraged each other, vented, and lamented. I shared my crazy Russian spy theories with her, and she was a shining example of what true empathy looked like. Whenever one of us found a program, article, video, or resource that we found helpful, we shared it with one another. Amy took it a step further by gathering all the info along the way and organizing it on a Trello board. If I was struggling with something, she would often send me a snippet or article she had already read and she knew it was spot on to what I was dealing with.

We finally got to meet in person at her place during a retreat with other midlife crisis wives and that's where I met Grace. We three hit it off like it had always been written in the stars. I even had the opportunity to meet up with Grace a couple weeks later when I realized my husband's work trip was near her. Two years later, Grace and I went out again to visit Amy and the three of us had the best long weekend adventure together. This is one of those silver linings, these friendships forged during crazy times.

I say that I am no expert, as in I have no formal training as a coach or in education like Amy does, however if you count life experience, I definitely fit the bill when it comes to midlife crisis expertise. I've lived with the monstering, the distance, the complete change of character, the depression, the betrayal. I've looked inward to identify behavior patterns that weren't serving me. I worked hard to forgive current transgressions and past resentments. I stood for my marriage when most people would have thrown in the towel. So as this type of expert and as a close friend of Amy's, I say with complete confidence that this guide she has written is a lifeline for someone beginning this journey. This book is something we would have devoured and shared with one another. There are chapters we would definitely reread and cite while we discussed our situations. I am so incredibly proud of her, for both her big heart and passion for helping others along with producing content that is truly meaningful and well laid out. I also want to mention how brave she is, sharing her own personal stories and putting her name on her work. Many people producing content for midlife crisis or marriage issues who have gone through their own struggles are reluctant to put their real name out there because they don't want to hurt anyone in their circle. I know firsthand what a hard decision this was for Amy, as she is very protective about those she loves. In the end, she knew the book would resonate more by sharing her stories. I can't wait to see what she does next. She's just getting started!

Jennifer Goodman

INTRODUCTION

On Christmas Eve 2022, I received a ten-page letter from my husband. It was overflowing with love, devotion, and promises for our future. In his own words, I was the only person he could ever imagine spending his life with. It felt like a validation of everything we had built together. It felt safe. It felt real.

And then, without a warning, our marriage was over.

By February first, only a few months later, the man who had poured out his heart to me with promises of forever had suddenly changed and made up his mind:

His feelings were gone.

He never said a word.

No conversation.

No fighting.

No confession.

Just silence, as if our twenty-five years together had never existed.

On February 17th, he told me he wanted a divorce. A few days later, I was served with papers.

No explanation.

No kindness.

No warning.

Just cold, legal documents.

I was devastated.

This is midlife crisis.

This is the tsunami that rips through your life when you least expect it. It is not marriage problems. Marriage problems you see coming. Midlife crisis ambushes you.

This story was sent to me by email. Sadly, it's not rare. I've received many of them. Although the ending of a marriage doesn't always happen this quickly, the elements are often heartbreakingly similar.

It happens to women (and also men) everywhere, with different timelines and different details, but with the same raw betrayal, the same confusion, the same utter destruction.

Maybe you thought your marriage was solid too. You believed you had weathered the storms and built something strong, something lasting. You trusted the life you made together. You trusted him. You'd been married for so long, you felt like all the big issues had all been worked out. There were no major fights, no lingering doubts, just the comfort of a life you built together. You never even considered the possibility of your husband straying or wanting a different life. After all, you'd been together forever, and things felt, at least to you, very secure until…

One day, out of the blue, your husband said:

"I love you, but I'm not in love with you."

Or maybe:

"You're great, but I just want something different. We no longer have anything in common."

Or even:

"My feelings about you have changed."

Perhaps he even dropped this bombshell: "I want a divorce."

Does any of this sound familiar? If it does, you're not crazy. You're not alone. You're just living through a nightmare that has a name: midlife crisis.

Men in midlife crisis often use the same chilling phrases, almost like they're following the same playbook. For spouses experiencing this behavior, it's devastating. If you're here, reading this, it means you're trying to survive the unimaginable. And you will. I promise you—you will survive this.

My clients are amazed when I rattle off these phrases because they think they are the only ones who have heard them. They're shocked to learn that men in midlife crisis often say the exact same things, sometimes almost word for word. What's equally shocking is the commonality of spouses being able to answer yes to any (or all) of these questions:

- Have you been married fifteen years or more?
- Do you feel like you're walking on eggshells with your spouse, blaming his anger and depression on his job?
- Has your husband moved out or is he talking about moving out?
- Has your husband lost a parent or best friend in the last few years?
- Are you empty nesters?

Welcome, dear friend. You are likely at the early stages of your husband's midlife crisis (MLC). I know this isn't easy to hear but bear with me throughout this book and be open. You are not alone, and you are not powerless.

In this book, you will learn:

- Why your husband is acting so differently and what's really going on in his mind.
- What midlife crisis really is.
- How to navigate your husband's behavior without losing yourself.

- How to respond (and not respond) to his behavior to avoid making things worse.

- Proven strategies to help you regain your confidence, manage your emotions, and find clarity.

I know it sucks to be here. I'm sure you never thought you would be here. It's not fair. You didn't ask for this. You've done everything you know to avoid this, or never even thought about it. But here you are. Like you, I never thought I'd be where you are now, and I never imagined writing a book about it. Being caught in the throes of your husband's midlife crisis is an earth-shattering experience. There just isn't another way to explain it. It affects every area of your life, from your career or business to your children, relatives, social life, finances, health, and more. But life does get better, I promise. Even though you might not believe it right now, even though it feels like there's no chance the husband you married will return, chances are good that he will.

When my husband first started going through his MLC, I knew something was wrong. He wasn't himself. I honestly thought he had a brain tumor. The change completely blindsided me. I didn't even know what to search for online to try to find a solution. I looked up *male depression* and later, *how to save my marriage.* I had no clue that my husband was in an MLC. When I finally realized his behavior was an MLC, I was so relieved that there was a name to it and that I wasn't crazy. But I didn't know at the time what MLC meant.

This crisis is a journey for both of you, but it's not about the marriage, it's about your spouse and his unhappiness with his life. Midlife crisis isn't a reaction to you; it's an internal battle he's fighting with himself. Right now, he may seem like a stranger: distant, irritable, even reckless. You might be searching for ways to fix things or wondering what you did wrong. But here's the truth: This is his storm to weather, not yours to control. You can't fix this.

What you can control is how you navigate this crisis for yourself, protecting your peace, finding clarity, and making choices that support you. And that's exactly what this book will help you do.

Experiencing your husband's MLC is like being on a roller coaster you never agreed to ride. Your emotions swing wildly—anger, confusion, fear, and heartache—and you feel powerless. You didn't sign up for this ride, but you're stuck on it, clinging to the sides, bracing for the next drop. It's hard to make sense of things in the beginning. You question everything: your relationship, your self-worth, your future. You wonder if you caused this. And just like a roller coaster's twists and turns, your husband's behavior is erratic. Sometimes he's the man you married, and other times he's a stranger. It's exhausting.

Here's the thing: Once you get off the roller coaster and step back, you'll see things more clearly. You'll observe the ride instead of being consumed by it. This new perspective will give you the clarity and strength to move forward, to build a life that's true to you, whether or not your husband returns to the marriage.

So, how do you stand for your marriage when your husband has left mentally, emotionally, or physically? How do you react when he doesn't seem to care about the marriage or the years you've spent together? What do you do when you know something is deeply wrong with him, down to your bones? How do you get through this?

Well, my friend, it's going to be ok. I've got you. You need a guide. You started this journey unprepared, devastated, embarrassed, and scared. You had no idea what you would need to navigate this path. As you embark on it, you will realize that it's a long journey with shifting terrain. Your friends and family might not understand or know how to support you. Unless someone has gone through this, they have no idea what it's like. Well-meaning friends may try to help, but often their advice misses the mark.

That's where I come in. As a wife who has firsthand experience with a husband going through MLC, I will help you navigate this storm. Everything in this book comes from my own journey, from my friends who have also gone through this, from my work with countless women facing the same challenges, and deep research into the psychology of MLC, relationships, and emotional resilience.

A lot of people don't agree with me about standing for your marriage and the process it takes to do so. They just think my husband is a jerk and we didn't have a good marriage in the first place. But we did. I know one day MLC will be categorized and recognized as an emotional disorder. Too many people go through it. They are in a fog and later wake up and wonder what the heck happened. My purpose isn't to prove MLC is real. My purpose is to help other women understand they are not alone.

For more than five years, I have researched the topic of MLC. What I have learned is both shocking and insightful. Now, I'm here to educate and support you through this challenging time. What I share comes from the trenches—my own and those of the brave women I've walked beside. My friend, I was once crying uncontrollably on the bathroom floor. I vowed that when I got to a better place emotionally, I would help others going through this. So here I am, ready to guide you. It's a long road with valleys, hills, and mountains. Every obstacle you face will teach you something new about yourself. In the end, you'll come out stronger and own your happiness. Over time, you'll emerge, battered but whole, and it's so worth it.

You can survive this. Stand for your marriage and even thrive. I believe in you!

Chapter 1.

GROUND ZERO: BOMB DROP "I LOVE YOU, BUT I'M NOT IN LOVE WITH YOU"

And just like that, the life I thought I had, unraveled in a single sentence.

~Anonymous

I never saw it coming. Most people don't. My husband was the Boy Scout. Everyone around us (including me) would have bet money on us being together forever.

My husband had recently changed jobs. He took a month off between them. To me, it seemed the month he was off was the happiest he had ever been. We had so much fun entertaining family, enjoying cookouts, welcoming family into our home. Those were great times spent together. So, when his demeanor changed suddenly a month after he began his new job, I assumed it was due to stress over the job and his new coworkers. He seemed angry all the time, unhappy, and withdrawn. He also started a keto diet, and I thought maybe his crabbiness was just a phase. He was irritated with everyone (not just me) and angry about everything all the time.

I wanted to blame it on COVID, but this started months before the pandemic hit. COVID just made it worse—way worse.

He began taking long walks, listening to music, and disappearing for hours. He dove into woodworking. He even tried therapy, which was a big step for him. Like many husbands, he wasn't the type to admit he might need help. He started mentoring a kid, working out, and going to the gym. He was trying to figure himself out but was clearly struggling. He volunteered to rebuild my best friend's trellis and began helping her move furniture for her business. His anger and irritability grew worse. I felt like I was walking on eggshells. I wanted to help him, to talk things out the way we always had. But he didn't know what was wrong, didn't want to talk, and gradually, he didn't want to spend time with me anymore. I don't know the actual date he dropped the bomb, but his words struck me to the core. Only then did I realize our marriage was at stake.

It was a Sunday morning. I was in the kitchen unloading the dishwasher when he said it. I don't even remember the conversation, I thought everything was fairly normal in our lives... until it wasn't.

Out of the blue he just said, "I love you, but I'm not in love with you."

That's when I knew something was majorly wrong. Before that, I thought it was just work stress and pandemic blues. While I want to tell you what prompted him to say that and what I said next, I really have no idea. The conversation was all a blur. I think I went upstairs. I was in shock. It's like when you get into a car accident and you have no idea what happened. Your mind goes blank. You don't remember any of the details. In the moment, I thought the depression he had been exhibiting had something to do with me. Later, I learned it wasn't about me, but at that moment, I thought I was the cause.

That phrase, "I love you, but I'm not in love with you," sent my body into a tailspin. I had an instant flare-up of rheumatoid arthritis (RA) that had been in remission for ten years. My ankle swelled, and I could barely walk. I blamed it on the gym at first, but when the swelling moved to other joints, I knew the RA was back, and I knew why. I felt alone and depressed. I couldn't talk to anyone. My mom and mother-in-law knew something was wrong, but I let them think it was just my illness. I couldn't tell them the real reason for the flare-up. My husband also knew the connection between the flare-up and what he had said, and he felt horrible about causing it. At times, he was sweet and understanding. He even waited a whole year to move out until I was back on medication and could walk again. But once my RA was under control and our son moved back home, my husband moved out. I was devastated. A few months later, he was seen with my (former) best friend, and they officially began dating.

And so began my journey of standing for my marriage and surviving my husband's MLC. I didn't have a clue what it was until I stumbled across an article about the stages of MLC and recognized my husband's behavior. That's when I realized MLC isn't what most people think. It's not about affairs or fancy cars. Those are just symptoms. That was the first bomb drop in my husband's MLC experience, and it was a doozy for me.

Bomb drop is the moment the MLC stops being a quiet storm in your husband's head and it explodes, spilling chaos all over your life. This is where the journey begins for the standing spouse, the left behind spouse who chooses to stand for her marriage. Until then, you know something is off, not right, or wrong. You can't pinpoint it exactly, you just know something isn't quite right. Your husband is distant, irritable, and unhappy. Maybe he's made some odd comments about feeling trapped or wanting more. But you brush it off, telling yourself he's just stressed. You never imagine he thinks it's about the marriage. Then, suddenly, BOOM! He says, "I love you, but I'm not in love with you." Or maybe it's, "I'm moving out," or "I don't think I ever really loved you," or "I want a divorce." Whatever it is, a bomb drop hits you like a freight train, leaving you disoriented

3

and scrambling for answers. This is the first term in the "Dictionary of MLC Language" that you will learn.

Every MLC journey has at least one bomb drop, a defining moment that instantly changes everything you once thought was true about your marriage. It's relationship news that you don't see coming and it shocks you. It's the moment the reality of your marriage shifts forever. Bomb drop can come in two ways: 1) a statement he makes, or 2) something he gets caught doing by you or someone else.

Before we go any further, I want to explain a few more terms you will need to know. MLC has its own language and terminology. Most people don't know these terms. I had to learn them by asking because there wasn't a place where they were all listed. If you've spent any time in MLC support groups or forums, you've probably seen this unfamiliar language. (If you don't know where or what those groups are, don't worry, I'll explain that later in Chapter Six.) These terms, which you will see throughout this book, sound like a mix of psychology, self-help, and internet shorthand.

- MLC: Midlife Crisis.
- MLCer: Person going through the crisis.
- BD: Bomb Drop: The defining moment you know your marriage is in trouble.
- DT: Duct Tape: This means don't say anything, keep your mouth shut; from Laura Doyle's books. We'll talk more about her later.
- LBS: Left behind spouse: The spouse not in crisis. (I hate this term, but it's everywhere, thus the reason I use it in this book.)
- LD: Laura Doyle: Author of *The Surrendered Wife*, *The Empowered Wife*. You will see it in MLC groups as "Use LD," which means use her principles.

- GOFL: Goddess of Fun and Light. Be yourself, be happy, go with the flow, as Laura Doyle says.

- OW: Other Woman or the affair partner.

- OM: Other Man or the affair partner.

- Pain shopping: Looking through your spouse's social media, driving by the affair partner's house to see if your spouse is there, or anything you go looking for that causes you pain.

- HB: Hearts Blessing: A pioneer in MLC. You'll learn more about her soon.

- Midlife Crisis Playbook (MLC playbook): This is not actually a book, but it means common things MLCers do or say.

- Monstering: When your spouse says mean things to you, tries to start an argument, or is combative and verbally abusive.

- The Tunnel: For the MLCer it's all about them in their own world. They are "in the fog" where they can't see what they're doing to everyone around them. Eventually they come out of the tunnel.

- Serial cheater: These are men (or women) who lack morals and like sleeping with others with no strings attached. Often, they have done this early in the marriage. This is different from MLC.

- Standing spouse. The person who chooses to hold space for their husband in MLC, while continuing to grow and move forward with her life.

- Exit affair: Men (or women) who fall in love with an affair partner, move on from the marriage, and don't look back. This is different from an MLCer. This is also different from "limerence," which is a temporary state of perceived love.

Some of these terms will make you nod in recognition, while some might sting a little, and a few might make you roll your eyes. Knowing this language will help you understand the ideas in this book better, help you make sense of what's happening, and help you realize you aren't alone. Now that we have the MLC terms out of the way, let's continue our conversation about bomb drops.

Bomb Drop Statement

The bomb drop statement is very common. It's an unexpected, intentional, out of the blue statement your husband makes about your marriage, about you, or about your lifestyle with him. My bomb drop was one a lot of women hear: "I love you, but I'm not in love with you."

This is such a common phrase in the MLC playbook that there is even a book with that title, *I Love You, But I'm Not In Love With You.*[1] However, it could easily be replaced by another common phrase such as: "My feelings have changed," "I need space," "I'm moving out," or "I want a divorce." Whatever the bomb drop statement, most spouses do not expect it and, therefore, are left feeling as if their world has been crushed. Thus, the bomb. One woman told me her bomb drop happened after her husband came home from a work trip and said, "I don't know when the last time was that I was happy." She didn't know until that moment that something was very wrong. A few weeks later, he also used the phrase, "I love you, but I'm not in love with you."

Bomb drop is such a defining moment in the MLC world that in many MLC discussion groups, people share their "BD (bomb drop), years married, and separation date" to indicate their experience. It is the start date for the left behind spouse's journey. There can be other bomb drops along the way, but the first one is the start date; you just might not realize it at the time.

Months after my husband dropped the first bomb, he shocked me again with another one by saying, "We'll just get divorced and be best friends." My mouth dropped wide open, and I thought, *WTF? Divorced? We went from happily married, building a house together, celebrating our twentieth anniversary a few years ago, and going on exotic trips... to this? And, no! I don't want to be best friends with you if that happens. Who does that?* I didn't say a word. It was like a car accident. I didn't know what I did or how this sudden thing happened, I was so in shock. I didn't tell anyone. There was no one to tell. I couldn't tell my parents, his parents, or our friends because I was taught to always keep my marriage private.

In my mind, we had the perfect marriage. We didn't argue. We even had date nights every week. But at that moment, I knew something was off, not with our marriage, but with my husband. We weren't fighting, he just said these things matter-of-factly. And I looked at him like he was crazy because I thought he was.

He even told me, "I don't think you are the love of my life; I think that was Sherry (not her real name)," a woman he dated for five years before we knew each other. By the time he said this to me we had been together for more than twenty years. So, where was this coming from? If she was the love of his life, why had he been with me all of those years? It didn't make sense to me, and he couldn't even explain it.

So, those were my bomb drops. And the thing to note about them is that they don't come with a warning. They hit you like a truck, leaving you stunned, confused, and trying to make sense of a new reality you didn't sign up for.

Here are a few more you might have heard:

- "I haven't been happy in a long time."
- "We had a good run."
- "I'll always love you; I want us to still be friends."
- "I don't love you the same way anymore."
- "I will always love you because you're the mother of my kids."
- "I don't know if I want to be married anymore."

Bomb Drop Incident

Bomb drops can also come in the form of an incident. One MLC spouse survivor shared one of hers that happened on New Year's Eve. Her husband accidentally posted to their Snapchat friend group instead of to the person he had been having an affair with: "I love you, Vickie." Everyone in the group saw the post. She was devastated and angry. When she asked her husband, "Who the hell is Vickie?" he tried to pass it off as a joke between him and an old friend. She offered to call the friend to verify the story, and her husband said, "Let's talk about this tomorrow morning," because they had company. The next morning, he tried again to avoid admitting the affair, but he finally did. "She's someone I met online." Later, many of the friends in their group who had seen the husband's post sent condolences to the wife. Of course, none of that helped to ease the pain and embarrassment she felt.

The bomb drop incident can also be news from someone else. Some wives have discovered their husband has cheated on them because someone reports that they saw him with another woman. That news is also a defining moment.

The Emotional Fallout of Bomb Drop

Chances are pretty good if you are reading this book, that bomb drop has already happened to you, because you likely didn't have a clue before this. Like me and most wives, you were blindsided. You thought everything was fine in your marriage until bomb drop. Once it happened your world was shaken, you were confused, and you felt all alone. So, let's talk about the emotional earthquake of feelings you are probably feeling right now.

***Feeling like your marriage is over doesn't
mean that it is.***

The thing is, a bomb drop doesn't just shake up your marriage, it also shakes and crumbles your entire sense of security, identity, and future. It feels like the rug has been pulled out from under you. At first you are so stunned you might feel:

Shock. "Did he really just say that?"

Numb. "I don't even know what to feel."

Fear. "What will happen to me? What about our family?"

Grief. "I thought we were happy." "What happens now?" "Who will I grow old with?"

What you're feeling is totally normal. And what can make it so overwhelming is that you can feel all of these feelings, all at once. Even still, you might not realize what you are dealing with is MLC; I know I didn't. After the reality sets in that something is really wrong and the future of your marriage and family are at stake, you might feel:

Betrayal. "How could he do this to me after all of these years?"

Anger. "What the hell is wrong with him?"

Paralyzed. You feel unable to do anything.

Indecisive. You are unsure what to do next.

Terrified. "What happens now?"

Crazy. "How did I not see this coming?" "Where have I been?" (I assure you; you are not crazy.)

You are absolutely allowed to feel it all. Humans naturally try to avoid negative emotions because of the discomfort, but don't be afraid to feel it all. Sit with your emotions; they can't hurt you. I know it may not feel true right now. Feeling your emotions doesn't make you weak, it makes you human. And feeling like your marriage is over doesn't mean that it is. Your brain is just trying to process it all right now.

This is how the MLC story often begins. It feels like a personal attack on you, but it's not.

You're Not Alone in This

After bomb drop happens, you feel so alone. The person who would typically comfort you in such an emotionally strained time is the one who dropped the bomb on you. Now what?

Who to Turn to for Support

You don't have to navigate this alone. There are people and resources that can help you get through this.

- An MLC Coach or MLC therapist. This person should really understand MLC. Unfortunately, not all coaches and therapists understand how to deal with MLC. They may say they know how, but all too often they know about relationships and marriages; however, MLC is a totally different animal. Check out my support page on my website: www.standingspouses.com.

- Midlife Crisis Support Groups. There are many groups. For support from my Standing Spouses Private Facebook Group, visit:

  https://www.facebook.com/groups/standingspouses.

- Trusted family members and friends **who have been through this and know about MLC.** The key word is "trusted." Choose people who will listen without pushing their own agenda, judging, or telling you what to do.

Who Not to Talk To

- Your husband. Right now, he is not your emotional support system. Trying to seek comfort from him will do more damage than good. It could push him away and lead to more hurt.

- The other woman (if there is one). No explanation needed. Nothing good will come from this.

- People who shame or pressure you. Whether it's someone telling you to "Just move on," or to "Get over it," or "Maybe you're imagining things," or even that "Things will work themselves out," avoid those who invalidate your feelings or push their own opinions too hard.

One critical fact about bomb drop is that it's not about you, even if it feels like it is. That might be hard to believe right now. When the man who promised to love you forever suddenly pulls away, says he doesn't love you anymore, or even leaves, it feels intensely personal. It feels like a rejection of everything you are: your love, your worth, your history together. But this is not a reflection of you. It's a reflection of him and the storm he is going through inside himself.

Midlife crisis makes a man question everything, and unfortunately, you—his wife, his mirror—become the easiest person to blame. But that doesn't make his crisis your fault, and it doesn't mean you are unworthy of love, respect, or happiness. You are still you, even if he can't see that right now. More importantly, you are not alone. There is an entire community of women who have been blindsided by this, just like you have. We know the shock, the pain, and the confusion that comes with MLC. Everyone else thinks you should have seen this coming, but people like us, who have been there, know you didn't. We also know this: You will get through this. You will find strength, clarity, and healing.

Before I share more of my story, I want you to remember one thing: This book isn't just about what happened to me; it's about helping you heal. I'm here to walk this journey with you, to help you navigate the heartbreak, and to show you that no matter how lost you feel right now, there is hope.

When my husband said that phrase, "I love you, but I'm not in love with you," I was so devastated, confused, and shocked, that it seemed like the foundation of my life crumbled in that very moment. All I could think about was, *how did this happen? We have the perfect marriage!* We really did, or, at least, I thought we did. We had been married for twenty-two years at the time of bomb drop, and together for twenty-four years. What had I missed? What had I done wrong? As I experienced the journey of MLC, I learned the answer to both questions. Nothing.

I thought the problem was me. I thought I had done something to push him away. I spent more than a year vacillating over my possible mistakes and how I had missed the fact that my husband was so unhappy in our marriage. Had I neglected him? Was I too naggy, too boring? Had I failed to see the warning signs? Or was it something else entirely, something he had been carrying all along that had nothing to do with me? Each time I came up with different possibilities of the things I might have done to jeopardize my marriage, and each time, I came up empty. Of course, I wasn't a perfect wife, but I felt I was pretty good. Just like most wives, I did my best to give my husband emotional support when needed, physical attention, shared responsibilities around the house and in our finances, in addition to doing the traditional gender roles of a wife.

Not until I came across a website with tons of research that explained my husband's behavior, did I realize he was in an MLC and it wasn't about me. All of this weirdness actually had a name if I could take myself out of it. Once I settled into the truth that the problem was not me, I became fascinated by the information I uncovered. All of my research confirmed the fact that it was a major MLC, an emotional, psychological, and hormonal experience he was having. Midlife crisis looked completely different from anything I could have imagined. I learned that it is not about sports cars and affairs. Those are just symptoms the media portrays.

For most men, the turmoil they exhibit has probably been brewing for a while, but you just didn't know it. It's not about how you fold the laundry, or your cooking, or how your body has changed since you got married. It's about the inner chaos inside your husband's brain that whispers to him, "Am I still relevant?" With that, he begins to seek the answer. Everything within him—his hormones, thoughts, emotions, and more—searches for evidence that he is, in fact, relevant.

What Not to Do

After I realized my husband was in MLC, one of the first things I wanted to know was why. It didn't take long for me to realize that he didn't know why. He didn't even know what was happening. So, I had to think deeply about how I would approach him going forward. Through lots of trial and error, I learned some very important things not to do:

1. Don't interrogate him.
2. Don't beg or plead.
3. Don't try to make him feel guilty.
4. Don't try to fix it.
5. Don't point it out.
6. Don't freak out.

Don't interrogate him. It didn't take long for me to realize that any line of questioning I had for him only made matters worse. It put him more on edge and caused him to be more distant. He really didn't know what was wrong. He likely received my interrogative questions as a form of pleading and irritation. And that is the last thing you want to do.

Don't beg or plead. Among the numerous behaviors you don't want to exhibit after bomb drop is begging and pleading. He is self-focused and has already justified his mindset. His world has shrunk to what he feels, what he wants, and what he thinks will make him happy. He's using his survival brain. Right now, he is looking for reasons to justify his decision to pull away from you. If you beg or plead, you unknowingly give him those reasons. Your emotional pleas may make him feel more trapped than he already feels. He is only thinking of himself at this point, so any pleading on your part will only confirm to him that he is making the right decision. Although he might feel sorry for you, his propensity for empathy or deep emotional concern for you is slim.

Don't try to make him feel guilty. Feeling guilty often leads to the MLC husband running away and never wanting to return. At this point, he is already drowning in a whirlwind of conflicting emotions. Deep down, he knows that what he's doing is hurtful, although he might not fully admit it to himself. Trying to make him feel guilty—whether through reminders of the life you've built together, the pain he's causing you, or the impact on the kids—only triggers his flight response. Guilt doesn't lead to reconciliation. Rather, it leads to avoidance. He has all these negative thoughts running through his mind. He thinks he wants to leave because of you. He thinks he has made up his mind, but he doesn't know he's in an MLC. If he feels guilty, he won't think, "I should fix this and come back." Instead, he'll think, "I can't handle this pressure. I need to escape even more."

Instead of facing his feelings, he will:

- Justify his actions further ("I had no choice. She made me miserable.").

- Look for distractions, such as affairs, new hobbies, or reckless decisions.
- Distance himself emotionally so he doesn't have to feel his guilt.

The harder you try to make him see how much he's hurting you, the more you'll push him deeper into the crisis, and convincing himself that leaving is the only way to escape and find happiness.

Don't try to fix it. Most men in MLC don't know they are in crisis until after the crisis is over. Even then, some don't realize how significant it was or the damage they have caused to their family, their career, their finances, and more. They just know they aren't happy, and they want to blame you and the marriage. It doesn't matter what you say. By the time bomb drop hits, he has convinced himself that he is done with life as he has known it and he is ready to move on with his life... without you. He wants to move out. He doesn't want to work on the marriage.

As hard as it might be, do not try to fix the situation. You didn't create it, so it isn't yours to fix. He is not in the mental state to solve the problem; he just wants something else, even if he doesn't know what that is. Any effort you make to engage in relationship talk right now will fall on deaf ears and likely frustrate him. In his mind, he's done. No amount of trying to convince him right now will work.

Do not suggest attending marriage counseling together. Most of my clients who try couples counseling find that this immediately backfires. The reason couples counseling doesn't work is because the MLC isn't about the marriage, it's about his crisis. Individual therapy is fine, but again, you cannot suggest it. You can't suggest anything. He doesn't want anything from you.

Don't point out the MLC. Unfortunately, telling your husband that you think he is having an MLC isn't helpful. I tried explaining to my husband what I was seeing: a confused man going through a crisis. When I showed him the research, I thought it would fix everything. He listened, but then got angry and said, "That's not what's going on." At that point, he shut down. A few days later, he asked to see the MLC research I had mentioned, and I showed it to him, but we never spoke of it again. He later told my oldest son, "Mom thinks I'm having a midlife crisis; maybe I am." Yet, on several occasions, he told me that wasn't the issue. Even in the throes of it, most men in MLC do not recognize what's going on. It's not until after they come out of the crisis years later that they realize what happened. One of my friends, who has gone through years of surviving MLC, told me her husband said, "You know, I think I went through something these last few years." She was a bit dumbfounded. "You think?" she said to me.

Don't freak out. This is easier said than done, right? Your husband just dropped a bomb on your life, and everything feels like it's spinning out of control. Your mind is racing with the worst-case scenarios: He's leaving forever. My marriage is over. My entire future just disappeared. The instinct to panic and take immediate action is completely normal. But panic leads to rash decisions.

Many women severely overreact after a bomb drop and go straight to a divorce attorney to file divorce papers. This isn't just anecdotal. Statistically speaking, women initiate divorce far more often than men, especially in midlife. "Women initiate divorce at age fifty and older—also known as gray divorce—in 66 percent of cases, according to research by AARP."[2]

Before you file papers, hit pause. Breathe and give yourself space. You've been together a long time, so don't rush this. Reflect on what might be motivating his behavior. Is this truly out of character, or could it be something deeper? Most importantly, does he sound like a sane person at the moment?

My husband had always been the do-gooder, "Boy Scout" type. His MLC behavior was a total 180-degree shift from his normal personality. This wasn't the same person I had met more than two decades earlier, whom I had loved all that time, and who had confided in me during some very difficult challenges in his life. I had to trust the relationship we had built over the years and realize that everything I was experiencing during MLC wasn't about me.

In the midst of trying not to freak out, you must acknowledge your own feelings. Yes, you are hurt, and you're allowed to be. But try to take your ego out of it. This is not about you. He is hurting, and he's lashing out. Since you are the closest person to him, unfortunately, you will bear the brunt of the attacks driven by his emotional pain. As the saying goes, "Hurt people, hurt people." His thoughts and actions belong to him. You don't have to own them or take responsibility or blame. They have nothing to do with you or with your marriage.

Despite all of that, you still want answers. But here's the thing: One of the biggest surprises of bomb drop is that your husband doesn't have any answers. He doesn't have a clue what's happening to him, so he can't help you understand. For the most part, whatever he says the reason is for feeling this way, probably isn't. With that, you need to do your best to keep your head on straight, guard your emotions, and find a way to respond. But how?

How to Respond to Bomb Drop Without Losing Your Mind

Most women react with a mixture of shock, confusion, anger, and panic after a bomb drop because they aren't expecting it. After I got over my initial shock, I tried everything—heart-to-heart talks with him, researching, reading, and more. But I didn't know what to look for. My first thought was, "How can I fix this?" I wanted to talk to him about what was going on, but he didn't want to. With my every attempt to communicate, he shut down even more, so I stopped

17

asking. I would hide out in my office, surfing the web and looking for answers. In those tortuous moments alone with my thoughts, I realized I literally had no idea what to do. The only thing I could do was write in my journal and research. When I don't know what to do, that's what I do; I write out my feelings and I research until things make sense. Information is power to me.

As I learned what not to do during my husband's MLC, I also discovered some actions that helped me manage the journey after my husband's bomb drop. Practice these:

1. Be quiet and listen.
2. Stop, breathe. You're going to be ok.
3. Manage your emotions.
4. Journal daily.
5. Write him a letter, but don't send it.
6. Be careful who you tell right now, because once you tell people, you can't un-tell them.
7. Research, research, research.

Some readers may not be ready for these actions, especially for those with trauma history. Talk to your therapist, as you may want to work on some grounding techniques and have an emergency self-care plan available.

Be quiet and listen. You want to fix this. You want to talk about it. You want to react and fight back and argue for your marriage. But this is not helpful. You can't reason with him in the MLC state. This will only make matters worse and push him even further away. So, instead, just listen.

He is experiencing an identity crisis where there is a huge gap between how he feels on the inside versus how he appears on the outside. It's called cognitive dissonance. As explained by Saul McLeod,

PhD in an article on SimplyPsychology.org,[3] cognitive dissonance is a psychological state where conflicting attitudes, beliefs, or behaviors produce a feeling of mental discomfort leading to a change in those attitudes, beliefs, or behaviors to reduce the discomfort and restore balance. Your husband can't explain it to himself, let alone to you. In all likelihood, he won't have much to say at all. He won't want to talk about his feelings or explain his actions and behaviors because he doesn't realize what's happening to him. So, do not ask him to explain himself, instead learn to listen to what he's not saying. Much like reading between the lines of a cryptic poem or looking for clues on the map for a scavenger hunt, you will need to practice hearing what isn't said. Listen for clues as to what is irritating your husband. He won't be specific or clear about his thoughts and actions, but he could drop hints and leave clues as to what's bothering him.

As you listen, take what he says with a grain of salt. Don't believe everything he says, especially when he speaks against you, attacks your marriage, minimizes the life you have built together, or tries to rewrite your shared history. In a MLC, he's not thinking clearly. He is trying to justify why he should leave, so creating a false narrative serves his needs. He may bring up small, petty grievances that happened so long ago that you didn't know they were even an issue. Let him get it out and do your best to remain calm. When the conversation becomes too much for you, tell him, "I need a minute," and step away. If he persists, then say, "I would like to continue the conversation at another time." Don't be surprised if he doesn't talk at all. Most MLC husbands don't want to talk about it. At all. Most avoid deep conversations like the plague.

It's hard not to notice his behavior, but don't fixate on it. Don't go looking for it. This is not an open door for you to become (or hire) a private detective and catch him in the act with another woman or to point out some lie or inconsistency in his explanation of where he has been or why he has done something. It's about recognizing that what's happening is about him, not about you. Let what you observe be quiet confirmation that you are not the problem. How well you detach and not fixate on his behavior will often determine how well you survive—and even thrive—through his MLC, so it's critical you don't watch his every move. The earlier you can detach from his behavior the better. We'll talk more about that.

Manage your emotions. Try to manage your emotions by not taking it all personally. I will admit that this is extremely difficult but doing your best to not take this personally could mean the difference between life and death for you. If you've had what you thought was a happy marriage, it's difficult to watch it crumble. This is your best friend, the one you thought you could trust to be there forever. The one who is now negating your entire marriage. The one who suddenly has turned on you. But you have to take "you" out of it right now. This is his crisis.

One of my coaches, Brooke Castillo, says, "Whatever someone says about you, you can usually find some truth in it, even if it's just 1 percent." So, remember this and stay calm. If your husband says some nasty things about you, while part of it may ring true for you because of that small percentage of truth, you do not have to believe him. Remember that on the other side of that 1 percent of truth is 99 percent false. If your husband says, "You are a bitch!" Don't believe him. You might think of instances where you were bitchy, but you know that is not your entire personality. If he says, "I hate your purple hair," and you don't have purple hair, would you believe him? Of course not. So, why would you believe everything he says when he lashes out and spews out garbage? Overall, keep your emotions in check because that is the one area that you can have one hundred percent control over. I realize keeping your emotions in check is especially hard right now, but keep reading, as I have more tips for this later.

Journal daily. When he's "monstering"—saying horrible things about and to you or behaving in a terrible way—journaling is a good way to get your emotions out. Write down all of your negative thoughts and feelings about him. Get it all on paper. Be "judgy." Use all the curse words you can think of if you like. Don't try to be nice or kind. Just let it rip! Obviously, don't share it with him; you don't want him to read it. This is a process to help you heal. It's for you, not for him.

Remember when you first met? Think about your thoughts and feelings back then. You have a choice about how you want to think and feel about him now. What if he said all of those things because he had cancer? What would you think about him now? Would you give him some grace or empathy? Remember, these are only your thoughts at the moment. Your thoughts control how you feel, and you have a choice in what you think. We always think our thoughts are true, but they are just how we choose to think about the situation. This is very important to remember. You have a choice in what you think.

Write a letter to him. Before I explain this part, let me be very clear. This is a letter for you, not for him. He is most likely not in a position to hear it or process it right now. **Do not share it with him.**

Here's what you'll do:

First pour out all of your thoughts on paper. Get it all out, no editing, no judging. Then, look at it, and ponder over it. After that, write a letter to him as if you are apologizing for everything you personally could have done better during your marriage.

Important: This does not mean that you caused his midlife crisis. His crisis is his responsibility. Midlife crisis is an internal, identity–driven struggle, not a direct reflection of your marriage or your worth. Even if he tries to blame the marriage, please understand this; his crisis is not about you.

The reason for writing this letter is to help you "clean up your side of the street" for your healing, not for his approval. It's a private exercise to take ownership and accountability of your faults and for self-reflection. Every marriage, even the best one, has room for growth. This is simply an opportunity to see where you want to grow, for your own sake, not because you are the reason for his actions. Doing this exercise also points out some of your own behaviors to pay attention to during his MLC.

When my husband first moved out, I wrote a letter and gave it to him. It fell on deaf ears and blind eyes. He didn't want to hear any of it. He was not in a position to absorb any of my emotions and insights. His response, "You've done nothing wrong. It's not you, it's me." I hoped something good would come of the letter, but nothing changed because again, an MLC is not about the marriage. Even if he says it is, it's not. Still, writing the letter helped me. It opened my eyes to small things I wanted to change in myself, not to win him back but to become the woman I wanted to be. I worked on those areas during his crisis, and over time, I didn't just become better, I became more loving and accepting of myself.

Who's at Fault?

Your husband's progression through an MLC is his issue, and his alone. Marriage problems are about the dynamics between two people, while MLC is about one person's internal turmoil. The spouse is not the cause. It's about the MLCer's struggle with themselves. You could have been the perfect spouse, and he still would have spiraled into crisis. Whether you were having challenges in your marriage or not, you are not at fault for the MLC. Often, MLC husbands accuse their wives of being the cause of the behavior they exhibit, especially if they choose to leave the home or marriage.

During your husband's MLC, he is looking to justify his behavior. In order to justify it, he makes you out as the bad guy.

This is where life coach Brooke Castillo's concept of Emotional Childhood vs. Emotional Adulthood comes into play.[4] As Castillo explains, in Emotional Childhood, adults have not matured past childhood patterns when it comes to managing their emotions. Instead of taking responsibility for how they feel, they blame others. This behavior is connected to something called, "self-serving bias," a distorted thought process where people protect their ego by blaming external circumstances for negative outcomes.

If something negative happens, they tend to believe the outcome is due to "situations or forces beyond their control." The self-serving bias is a falsified view that protects their ego.[5] For your MLC husband, there has to be negativity to support his negativity. Whether it's true or not, he will find or invent evidence to justify leaving because his mind needs a reason. If you are nice and kind, it will be harder for him to find that evidence, but don't be surprised if he twists things anyway. The important thing is that you'll know you acted with integrity, and you will have no regrets.

One left behind spouse told me, "I felt like I was walking on eggshells, and I couldn't be me. If I acted my normal way in a disagreement, that was building his case. Even asking questions, like, 'How was your day,' or 'What did you have for lunch?' was turned and twisted into a brash comment such as, 'Is this the Spanish Inquisition?' It was seen as demanding, inquisitive, and irritating. So were texts like, 'How was your day?' or 'How did the meeting go?' He was irritated by just the fact I existed."

No People-Pleasing

When you're being attacked or blamed unfairly, it's natural to want to defend yourself, or to try. You might find yourself walking on eggshells, doing special things, making nice dinners, or buying him gifts, all in hopes that you can somehow make it better, or fix it. This is where the trap of people-pleasing comes in.

You go overboard by doing things you think will make him happy because you want him to be happy. You want to go back to your old marriage when things were good. Although you think you are making progress to reconnect with him, you are actually exhibiting people-pleasing behaviors. And people-pleasing is a fear response. So, when you catch yourself doing things just to please him, realize that fear is the reason. I didn't recognize my people-pleasing until much later in my journey. And when I did, I didn't realize the reason for them was fear.

At this time and stage of the game, nothing you do will work if he wants to leave; you can't stop him. Doing nothing is extremely difficult, but if you try and stop him from leaving, it won't work. Keep reminding yourself that this is not about you. Keep reading and researching. I'll explain more in the next chapter.

What to Do Now

When bomb drop hits, your first instinct is to react, but staying calm is your greatest strength. Acknowledge your feelings, write them down in a journal, but don't unleash them on your husband. He is not in a position to hear it right now. Let him talk, just listen, and remember: His words reflect his current crisis mindset, not the objective truth. Avoid relationship discussions; he's likely looking for a fight and a reason to leave the marriage, and he will use anything you say to justify doing so. This isn't about you. Be kind, protect your peace, and keep reading for more to help you navigate this storm.

Key Takeaways

- Bomb drop is the start of your journey.
- This is not about you. This is about him.
- He can't explain what is happening to him because he doesn't know.
- Keep researching and learning.

Chapter 2.

MIDLIFE CRISIS—IT'S NOT WHAT YOU THINK IT IS: UNDERSTANDING THE JOURNEY

What a lot of people don't realize is that a midlife crisis goes way beyond sports cars, new clothing, and bimbos. It's a true crisis of identity.

~ Jennifer Goodman (Standing Spouse for five years.
Her husband came home still in MLC mode.
But now, they're emerging on the other side.)

After a bomb drop—after your world shatters—there is a strange disorienting moment when you realize you're still standing, but the landscape around you has completely changed. It's like finding yourself halfway up a mountain you never planned to climb, clutching at loose rocks, wondering how you got here and whether you'll ever find solid ground again. The husband you thought you knew, your steady climbing partner, has let go of the rope and vanished into the fog.

In this chapter, we're going to stop scrambling. We're going to map the mountain. Because understanding what MLC really is—and what it isn't—is the first step toward steadying yourself for the climb ahead.

More Than a Punchline

Most people really do not know about MLC, and what we think we know is only from movies, books, and social media. Midlife crisis often gets reduced to clichés.

The media has turned MLC into a punchline, an almost laughable stereotype of a middle-aged man buying a red convertible, dating a younger woman, or quitting his job to become a surf instructor. But when it happens to your husband, it feels nothing like a joke. It's painful, confusing, and life-altering. Your entire world crumbles. Midlife crisis isn't just about reckless decisions, and it's not something he'll simply "snap out of." It is a deep internal war, a struggle with identity, purpose, and unresolved wounds that have nothing to do with you.

The truth is, MLC isn't about what the media portrays. It is a full-blown identity crisis that wreaks havoc on your marriage, your family, and your sanity. But here's the good news: You can survive this and even thrive during this time. I understand the heartbreak of a left behind spouse all too well. When MLC came crashing into my life, it didn't look like the stereotypes. I was in total shock that this could be my husband or my life. The experience was brutal. It was messy. It blindsided me in ways I thought I'd never recover from.

I Thought He Had a Brain Tumor

I spent a whole year in hell between my rheumatoid arthritis (RA) flare-up, dealing with my MLC husband, and COVID. I had never been that unhappy in my life. For a time, I couldn't walk without crutches, nor could I use my right hand. My husband did his best to be sympathetic, but my health only made matters worse between us. He hated feeling trapped by COVID and began taking long walks after working from home.

During that time, my youngest was in school outside the country, so it was just the two of us at home. I couldn't tell my parents or his parents what was going on with my marriage, so I just blamed it all on the RA whenever I talked to them. My mother-in-law was so supportive. She sent me cards every week, telling me to hang on. What she didn't know was that the stress of dealing with her son's MLC was the cause of my medical condition.

I know he did his best, but I could tell he was crawling out of his skin. He would play games on his phone for hours while watching TV, trying to avoid the negative thoughts in his mind. He was restless and angry. He lashed out at everyone. He took up new hobbies like woodworking and created beautiful pieces for me. He would walk for hours around our neighborhood trying to make himself feel better. But eventually it was all too much.

After being quarantined in his dorm room and facing challenges getting groceries, our son decided to come home from school. My husband jumped at the chance and decided to move out a few weeks later. By then, my medicine had started to work, giving me some relief from the RA symptoms. I think he felt better about leaving because he knew I wouldn't be alone, and the medicine was finally kicking in.

Up until then, I didn't understand what was going on with him. I had been doing a ton of research, but nothing made sense until I found the Hearts Blessing website (https://thestagesandlessonsofmidlife. org/sitemap/). That was my "aha" moment when all the pieces started to fit and I realized he was going through an MLC.

When my husband started acting differently, I thought he had a brain tumor. His behavior was so out of character for him. Even the smallest, most common things put him on defense. When I mentioned getting our youngest son a birthday present—something we usually chose together—he seemed irritated and said, "I'll get my own gift and card." Shocked, I backed off. He bought our son lavish gifts with a card and even a cute gift bag. Then, a few weeks later, on our oldest son's birthday, he showed up to pick us up to take us all out to a planned dinner. When he walked into the kitchen and saw all the gifts, he said, "Oh no! I forgot to get him a gift." I couldn't believe that only a few weeks before he went all out on our younger son and then did nothing for our oldest son. That was so not like him. He knew he was coming for a birthday dinner but didn't think of bringing a present or a card. "Don't worry," I said. "I already signed my card from both of us."

On another occasion, I overheard the kids and him talking about smoking cigars. He told them he had never smoked a cigar in his life. Both kids were surprised to hear him say that because we all knew he had smoked cigars on occasion with his good friend years earlier. Had he forgotten? Was he lying? And if so, why? It was so strange. He also suddenly started becoming a social person who drank, whereas before he was content to stay home and rarely drank. But the next two scenarios really stuck out in my mind and caused me to think he might have a brain tumor.

One day, after he had already moved out, he accompanied me to a surgery consult for melanoma on my face. I had planned to go alone or maybe take my youngest son since my husband didn't live with me anymore, but he wanted to go with me. It was nice to have him with me because the appointment was actually a big deal for me. After the consult, my husband suggested we go to lunch, which, again, was very nice but odd since he had moved out months before. He ordered a salad, like normal; I ordered a sandwich. After he started eating, I waited for him to give me his avocado, like he had for the last twenty years because he hates avocados and has hated them since I had known him. But what did he do? He ate the entire avocado half. My mouth hung wide open as I watched. Who is this guy? I said nothing. I was too stunned.

On another occasion, he mentioned going to a great Thai restaurant near his apartment. He hated Thai food, and we never went to those restaurants, although my son and I love Thai. I remember calling my aunt and telling her how bizarre his new eating behavior was.

"I think he needs an MRI," she told me. "Seriously, I think he has a brain tumor!"

I thought so too, but after doing so much research, everything I found pointed to MLC. I didn't tell her that, but by this point I was convinced.

These are just some of the many moments when I realized my husband wasn't the man I'd known. His personality, habits, and even his preferences were changing. Some changes were gradual; some seemed to happen overnight. It felt like a switch had flipped and I was left scrambling to understand what was happening. Was it stress? A brain tumor? The truth was much more complicated. After researching about MLC, I realized this bizarre change in his behavior was actually normal for an MLC husband. Personality change is the hallmark of MLC.

Looking back, I've realized there were subtle changes I didn't notice because I had no idea he was having an MLC. I knew something was horribly wrong, I just didn't know what. I also thought the changes could be because he was on a keto diet and maybe not getting enough carbs for his brain. I know! I was grasping at straws because he seemed to change so suddenly, almost overnight. Looking back, I can pinpoint more of those odd changes.

In the past, he always looked forward to family gatherings. Suddenly, he didn't enjoy being around family as much. On one trip to visit his cousins, everyone was having a great time, but he was preoccupied with reading an article on his phone even though we hadn't seen them in years. It was like he didn't want to be there. Later, I talked to his cousin about it, and she agreed that his behavior was weird. Still, I didn't know what to do about it.

Privacy seemed to be a big deal for him. Oddly, he started placing his phone faced down so I couldn't see notifications. Then, he changed the password on his phone. Before all of this began, he knew my password, and I knew his. He started closing the bathroom door whenever he went in when before, he never cared. There were times when he would suddenly decide to go out and wouldn't say where he was going. Most times when he would talk, which became more and more rare, the conversation was very vague. He didn't want to share anything with me. He seemed annoyed at watching our regular TV shows in the evening, almost as if he didn't want to be there. What became apparent to me was that he was so unhappy with his life and everyone around him. Even our sons had to find their own way of dealing with their dad. Years later, my son told me that during this time when my husband was acting so strangely, he just hid upstairs in his room because he didn't know what kind of mood Dad would be in.

For many spouses and their families, these behaviors are extremely difficult to understand and deal with. One of my friends said this about her MLC husband: "Looking back, the change was so gradual that it was under the radar for me. Not until he was irritated with me 24/7, for several weeks, did I realize something wasn't right. And yet, I still didn't think it was me, because it had never been me."

Understanding Midlife Crisis: Mapping Out the Terrain

If you feel like you're the only one facing this heartbreak in midlife, you're not. Divorces during this season of life, called gray divorces, have doubled since the 1990s. About one out of every three divorces today happen after the age of fifty.[6] How do you know that MLC is different from marriage problems, serial cheaters, or exit affairs? An obvious indicator is that what they do and say does not make sense to the average person, and it doesn't correlate with their normal personality. To the left behind spouse, it might seem like a split personality since this is not typical behavior of the person you know and love.

Some men may go through midlife transition, a natural phase of adult development and a time of self-reflection, which leads to positive changes like pursuing new hobbies or making healthier choices. An MLC isn't just a rough patch or stress; it's a complete identity overhaul. Many men experience it as they confront unresolved emotions. These emotions often stem from past regrets, fears about the future, unmet expectations, and major life changes.

Regrets could sound like:

- "Maybe I chose the wrong career. Did I play it safe instead of chasing my dreams?"
- "Did I marry the right person? Did I settle?"
- "Did I work too much and miss out on my kids' childhood?"

Fears might include:

- Aging and health issues: "I'm getting older. What if I get cancer or some other diagnosis?" Or maybe they do get a diagnosis and that scares them.
- Mortality: "My parents (or often best friend) just died. Am I next?"
- Financial security: "Do I have enough money to retire?"
- Being trapped: "Is this really all there is to life? Is there time to change it?"

Grief could be the result of:

- Death of a parent: Losing a parent often triggers deep reflection.
- Empty nest: Kids leave home and suddenly life feels empty and meaningless.
- Loss of youth and identity: Men often mourn their more confident selves, particularly when they see younger men in the workplace who seem to be taking their place, doing it better, faster, etc. They feel like the "old dogs."

Shame and Self-Doubt could be caused by:

- Weight gain and health decline: "I used to be fit and attractive."
- Past failures: "I should have done more with my life."
- Feeling like a disappointment: "I'm not the man I thought I would be."

Restlessness and Boredom might look like:

- Lack of excitement: "I need adventure. I feel like I'm suffocating. Life is boring at home."
- Desire to reclaim their lost youth: "This is my time." This often leads to reckless spending, sports cars, affairs, gambling, or extreme hobbies.

Resentment might stem from:

- Feeling unappreciated: "I've sacrificed everything for everyone else. Now it's my turn."
- Blaming the spouse: "My wife doesn't make me feel alive or happy anymore."
- Work burnout: "I've given my whole life to this job, and for what?"

These unresolved emotions often buildup over decades, and can also include other unresolved emotions from childhood, abuse, or PTSD. When multiple emotions hit all at once, the MLCer has no idea how to process them, so they act out impulsively instead. That's why so many MLC husbands seem to have a personality change overnight. While your husband's behavior may feel unpredictable and hurtful, it's important to remember this isn't about you. The MLC is usually not even about the marriage; it's about him going through something horrible.

In Kara Oh's book, *Male Midlife Crisis Why It Causes Men to Destroy Their Families, Finances and Even Commit Suicide, and What You Should Do,* she says, "Once you understand what it is all about, you will see how terribly insensitive all the jokes and teasing are. It is a serious and potentially devastating thing that men have to endure. The problem is that no one understands it, least of all the man who is going through it. And there is no preparation for its coming. All he knows is that he's dissatisfied with his life, feeling lost, alone and doesn't know why. And doesn't know what to do about it."[7]

I couldn't control his midlife crisis, but I could control how I responded to it.

If you ask your husband if he is going through an MLC, he will almost certainly deny it. Why? Partly because he doesn't really know what's going on and partly because he doesn't want to admit that something this huge and unknown is creating such discord in his life. "The irony is that the very reason men won't admit that they are struggling with an MLC is the same reason it occurs."[8] They have been taught from an early age to be "men" (e.g., "boys don't cry," "don't express your feelings.") Midlife crisis is seen as being weak. Men are conditioned to believe they are not allowed to be vulnerable, scared, express emotions, make any mistakes, or follow unconventional dreams.

I knew my husband was going through something terrible. I saw him fighting it, but there was nothing I could do. It was like a freight train he couldn't stop. He didn't want help from me. And now, after all the research I've done, I realize why: He didn't want to let me down. He didn't want to show me that vulnerable side of himself. He didn't know how to manage his feelings. Essentially, he had no idea what was wrong. Once I understood he couldn't fix it—and I couldn't fix it for him—I realized I had to shift my focus. I couldn't control his MLC, but I *could* control how I responded to it. That meant learning everything I could, not to fix him but to keep from falling apart. I needed to understand what was happening, why it was happening, and how I could survive it without going insane and losing myself in the process. What I discovered was altogether shocking, revealing, and comforting.

The Shocking Signs of Midlife Crisis (Who Is This Guy?)

Midlife crisis comes with some very telltale signs that are apparent once you learn to recognize them. But before that, you are confused by your husband's behavior. Sudden personality changes are often the first red flag, but they are not always as obvious as eating an avocado. Sometimes it's subtle, like a sudden obsession with their phone, avoiding eye contact, or snapping at you over little things. Other times, it's more drastic, like moving out, spending a ton of money on new hobbies, and even starting an affair.

Here is a checklist of common questions to ask yourself to determine whether your spouse may or may not be in MLC. I use this as a guideline. It's not a diagnostic checklist, but the more you check off, the greater the chance he is in MLC. MLC can happen at any time during a marriage. Most of the women I work with have been married more than fifteen years.

This is a short version of the MLC Checklist. For a longer version of this checklist, including explanations of these signs, go to: *https://www.standingspouses.com/free-checklist*.

- Have you been married/together fifteen years or more?
- Does he have any childhood trauma, such as sexual abuse as a child, child abuse that you know about?
- Has he lost a parent or a loved one recently?
- Has he changed jobs recently?
- Have your kids moved out recently?

- Is he moody, irritable, or angry most of the time?
- Does he lash out at you and accuse you of things, whereas he never did that before?
- Is he distant and withdrawn, no deep conversations, just yes and no answers?
- Does he make impulsive decisions, such as switching jobs, buying expensive items, or starting new hobbies or behaviors, such as gambling, drinking, or going to clubs?
- Does his behavior suddenly seem unrecognizable, even to his family (although, in the beginning, it may just be with you)?
- Is his behavior suddenly secretive?
- Does he accuse you of not wanting to have sex often enough?
- Does he have new friends and exclude you from their activities?
- Has he stopped doing activities and communicating with his old friends?
- Does he talk about getting older? For example, "Time is passing me by so quickly."
- Has he started working out, going to the gym, or is he suddenly obsessed with changing his appearance?
- Has he stopped wearing his wedding ring and blames it on sports, or working on the car, etc.?
- Does he seem to feel entitled to his new behavior?

Although these aren't all the signs, they're some of the clues that your husband might be in MLC. The hard part is that his behavior can feel like a rollercoaster. One day, he's distant, irritable, or acting completely out of character, and the next, he seems fine, almost like his old self. It's confusing and emotionally draining. You catch yourself thinking, *What's wrong with him?* And then dismiss it when things seem normal again. But over time, these moments of unpredictability become more frequent until you can't ignore them anymore. Reflecting on these patterns can help you recognize that what you're experiencing isn't your fault; it's part of the MLC playbook.

The MLC Playbook: A Set of Rules They All Seem to Follow

One surprising thing about MLC is how predictable it can be. Knowing what to look for is empowering and helps prevent you from feeling like you're going crazy or it's all your imagination or even accepting his blame for the resulting problems.

When I talk with other left behind spouses, we've all noticed the same or similar patterns. The men seem to follow an unspoken script in what they say and patterns in what they do—almost like they're all reading from the same playbook. While every man's experience is unique, this commonality is both baffling and oddly reassuring.

- There is always a bomb drop. This marks the start of the standing spouse's journey. But this isn't the beginning of the MLCer's journey. His started long before.

- A change in feelings toward the spouse. ("I love you but I'm not in love with you.") These feelings can quickly turn into disdain, loathing, or contempt.

- Total withdrawal from the spouse. He doesn't want to talk or engage and gives the silent treatment.

- Running away or avoidance. Behaviors such as never being home, not answering his cell phone, moving out, or starting an affair.

- Contradictory behavior. Engaging in actions that contradict his previous values or beliefs, rewriting the past in a way that feels inaccurate, and leaving the left behind spouse questioning the truth of what they hear.

Through countless hours digging into MLC groups and in my work with Standing Spouses, I have heard many stories that illustrate common traits, emotions, and experiences. What MLC spouses say and do during MLC often defies logic, leaving even their closest loved ones baffled. I've heard several stories where the MLCer encourages his spouse to find someone else. My own husband once said that to me: "You'll find someone soon," and mentioned a friend of ours who had remarried.

Here are a few stories that our group members have courageously shared. One woman I coach shared a conversation she had with her mother-in-law: "I told her I felt like something was wrong and that my husband had become a complete stranger—like an alien had taken over his body. He seemed dead inside. I even suspected he was seeing someone else."

Her mother-in-law responded, "I'm so glad you said that. I feel the exact same way. I don't even recognize him anymore." When asked how she knew her son might be seeing someone, the mother-in-law simply said, "Mother's intuition." Then she added, "I never imagined he would ever do something like this."

Another woman said this about her husband's new behavior: "He physically pushed a mutual (female) friend of ours. He pushed her face out of the way during a group FaceTime call because she kept interrupting him and hogging the screen. I thought she was going to kill him. He would have never done that before."

Once you know what MLC looks like, you may start to recognize it everywhere. Once you see it, you can't unsee it. Most people never recognize what it truly is unless they've been affected by it personally. The MLCer often moves throughout society seemingly unnoticed. They are leaders at work, physicians, military officers, bankers, tradesmen, presidents, and CEOs. A massage therapist once told me about someone she knew, who was a respected pillar of the community. He coached Little League. He was even the mayor at one point. But after the kids left home, he said, "I've taken care of everyone for so long, now it's time to take care of me." And what did "taking care of me" look like? He became a meth addict.

Midlife crisis is no joke. It can affect even the most put-together people you've ever met; those you'd never suspect would go through something like MLC. When I hear about famous or successful people on the news who have been married for a long time, and suddenly get divorced, I often wonder if it's an MLC.

Fortunately, many MLCers are good at compartmentalizing, so at first it may not affect their work. But as the crisis deepens, it often does, leading to job loss, financial ruin, and shattered families. Yet, because this isn't talked about openly, it largely goes unnoticed to the outside world, especially if there is no divorce. The real damage often stays hidden, visible only to those closest to him.

During these last few years, I met many men who had gone through MLC. No matter where they were from or what they did for a living, they all seemed to say similar things. Once, on a business trip, I met a man on a plane who sat next to me. He was friendly, about my age, and we got into a casual conversation about marriage. He asked what I did, and I told him I coached women going through their husband's MLC. He was very curious why I chose that career. As I explained a little of my story, he began to open up. As he did, the more obvious it became that he had gone through an MLC himself. His experience was textbook MLC. He and his wife were still living together but were divorced, something that happens quite a bit due to financial reasons or because they still want to stay close to their kids.

Many husbands do return home and to the marriage.

He told me, "I have four kids, and I still want to be part of their lives." He also explained that his wife had become so angry about his affair that she immediately filed for divorce. Unfortunately, this is all too common. I just listened to the man explain, "I just couldn't talk to her about this. I didn't really know what was wrong, but I just wasn't happy." He went on to say, "I'm supposed to be her rock, but I didn't want to look weak, and I really didn't know what was happening to me." I found it fascinating that he could actually tell me—a complete stranger—all about it.

He also didn't know why he did the things he did and hinted at childhood issues creeping up, but he just didn't know how to talk to his wife about it all. He said he had always been the sole provider, felt trapped in his job, couldn't see the future, and felt stuck in the day-to-day of life. He couldn't talk to his friends and tried counseling once, but it wasn't for him. He ended up in an affair, but the affair partner wasn't the fix either.

I said to him, "Usually the affair is just a distraction."

"You are right about that," he responded. "That's all she was, but I screwed everything up." He went on to explain that one day, he just "woke up and came out of a fog" (his words) and realized all he had lost. "I want my wife and family back, but she hates me for what I did. I don't think she'll ever take me back."

Many husbands do return home and to the marriage. Some couples even remarry if they divorced during the MLC. I find comfort in the fact that so many spouses return home because that means there is hope of reconnecting. I know of at least seven different homecomings among my own families and friends. Unfortunately, those stories are not openly discussed because when the husband comes home, he is ashamed, and the family is ashamed, yet relieved. Everyone just wants to forget the horror they've lived through, move on, start fresh, and pretend it never happened.

These stories highlight just how unpredictable and illogical MLC behavior can seem, even as it follows strangely similar patterns across different men. This consistency raises an important question.

If so many men seem to follow the same script, does MLC have defined stages or a common pathway?

Stages of a Midlife Crisis from a Spouse's Perspective: What He May Be Doing, What You May Be Feeling

There is no shortage of theories about the stages of MLC. Dr. Jim Conway, in his book *Men in Midlife Crisis*, linked them to Elizabeth Kübler-Ross's stages of grief, which were originally about terminal illness, not death. Another pioneer in this area, Hearts Blessing, developed her own stages.

When I first came across Hearts Blessing's work, it was like a lightbulb went on and illuminated my own path. Her descriptions perfectly captured what I was seeing in my own husband. Until then, I'd been completely in the dark. I was so excited that I even told my husband all about it. He wasn't thrilled. "No, that's not it," he said. But a few days later, he asked me to send him the information. We never spoke of it again. That's when I learned my lesson: Don't tell your husband he's having an MLC. While it's a relief for you to have a name for what's happening, he probably won't see it that way. He's unlikely to recognize it himself and, even after coming through it, he may not realize that's what it was.

Reading about these MLC stages helped me process what was happening. But it's important to acknowledge that the stages aren't a step-by-step map; they are not linear. They don't always follow a specific order, and they can overlap and occur at the same time. Some men might bounce between stages or even skip some entirely.

I've adapted Hearts Blessing's stages to help standing spouses like you.[9] These are meant as a guide, not a guarantee. Don't fall into the trap of thinking your husband is in a particular stage, so the next one means he's coming home. Every man's journey is unique. Some people do not find these stages helpful, but I did. That said, please don't take them as a guaranteed road map for what comes next for your husband. So many women in this situation get obsessed about the stages. These are just some of the behaviors you may be seeing.

If you want a deeper understanding, I recommend reading Hearts Blessing's work. Her insights are pure gold, the result of over twenty years of research. She was such a great authority and insight on MLC. I wish I could have met her before she passed away. While her perspective is religious, the value of her observations transcends any traditional religious beliefs, so I encourage you to focus on the insights, even if religion isn't your thing.

Midlife crisis typically strikes between the ages of thirty-five and fifty-five, though it can happen earlier or later. I've even had a client whose husband was only thirty-four when he began exhibiting MLC behaviors. A neighbor of my parents was in his seventies. While there are common patterns, no two midlife crises are exactly the same. And while this book focuses on men, women can experience MLC too, though women with MLC is discussed even less often.

Here are the stages of MLC from a spouse's perspective. Remember, these are things you might see, or you might not. Not every MLCer exhibits these behaviors and certainly not in a specific order. But many do; therefore, I have listed them here. Please do not obsess about them though.

Denial

You know something is wrong with your husband because he acts differently, but you don't know exactly why. He doesn't seem to enjoy things as much. You chalk it up to stress at work, changing jobs, tired of the daily routine, or exhaustion. He may or may not talk about getting older. He doesn't talk to you like he used to, or he's grouchy, crabby, and quiet. He starts looking at his phone or playing computer games all the time.

He's not fun anymore. He seems withdrawn. He can't look you in the eyes. You make excuses for him around other people. In my case, I later realized that he was being strong, not letting on that something inside was out of order or bothering him, and sticking to the strict code of masculine invulnerability. Some standing spouses may not even really notice this stage until they look back months later because their MLC spouse hides it well early on.

Anger

He is so irritable that you feel like you're constantly walking on eggshells. He won't look you in the eyes and avoids any close connection. You can't say or do anything right. He starts resenting you. He appears selfish and wants to get away from you. His comments are mean, and he may say nasty things without caring how it makes you feel. We call this behavior monstering. He may bring up old grievances that you never knew about. The kids learn to hide from him and stay out of the way. He appears to be consumed by angry thoughts. My husband told me he had so many bad thoughts running constantly through his brain that he turned to playing games, like sudoku, on his phone to distract his mind.

Your husband may be quite critical of you and want to argue over seemingly stupid stuff. He may talk about your family finances being "his money," and how much he has to do for this family and how no one seems to appreciate him. Some phrases you might hear him say include: "I need to live life for me now." "I'm sick of feeling trapped." "I'm not happy and I haven't been in a long time." "I feel like a paycheck, not a husband."

You may feel like he hates you and it seems to get worse every day. He blames you for everything. He tries to pick a fight and often, it's so he can say to himself, "See, she was a bitch, and I had to leave." It's his excuse to run away. This is the stage where he may start to think about moving out and talking about filing for divorce, although they can move out and talk about filing at any time. Bomb drop often occurs during this stage. As a spouse you are hurt, angry, confused and basically have no idea what is going on, but you know something is really wrong, and it has the potential to kill your marriage.

In the middle of all the anger and blame, one of the hardest things for me to witness wasn't the monstering, it was the way he no longer would look me in the eyes and the way his eyes changed. It was like the man I knew was vanishing right in front of me.

His eyes may look cold and black especially during the earlier years of MLC. It's striking to look back at old pictures of my husband and see how the light in his eyes gradually changed. Once warm and full of life, they became cold, hard, and vacant. In some social media groups, people have shared side-by-side photos of their husband's eyes. The transformation is undeniable. Before, during, and after the crisis something shifts, not just in behavior, but in the very expression of his face.

In my research on these dark, cold eyes, I've found no official scientific study directly linking them to MLC; however, several psychological concepts may help explain what is happening. When someone is under extreme stress, they can develop something called blunted affect, a reduced, emotional expressiveness that can make a person's eyes appear empty or lifeless. Emotional numbing, a common response to trauma or intense internal conflict, can also create a distant, detached look. Some men in crisis may even experience dissociation, mentally disconnecting from their emotions and identity, which can manifest as a vacant stare. And for some, a condition called alexithymia, or difficulty recognizing and processing emotions, can make their face almost unreadable.[10] Even the facial feedback hypothesis suggests that when someone suppresses their emotions over time, their facial expressions may dull, reinforcing the appearance of coldness.[11]

While these concepts don't specifically reference the dark MLC eyes, they help explain why so many women observe this eerie transformation. It's not just in your head; it points to a visible reflection of the emotional storm raging inside of him.

During this stage, it's best not to engage with their anger. Find your own activities and start doing more things on your own. He needs space so let him be.

Replay

The replay or selfish stage is "doing over their youth" or doing things he feels he missed out on. He acts like a teenager. It can look like he is having the time of his life doing a variety of things, including having affairs. Some even go back and look up their high school sweethearts.

This is the stage where he might turn to drugs, alcohol, gambling, or spending a lot of money, whereas before he wouldn't drink and might have been very frugal. He may start dressing better or more youthfully, even buying designer clothes. Some become obsessed with attending sporting events, concerts, and visiting casinos. Your husband may even change the way he speaks by using more swear words, slang, or youth language. Often, more hurtful behavior includes taking his affair partners on extravagant trips or experiences he never wanted to do with you. Spending holidays and special occasions with you and the family is hit or miss. He is gone a lot during this time.

Buffering is something you see in this replay stage. In general, humans naturally avoid negative emotions because we don't want to feel bad. Buffering is a way of escaping, not just your life but your mind and emotions. We buffer out negativity with things like eating, drinking alcohol, playing computer games, or shopping. The MLC husband is trying to avoid his negative emotions by buffering—with affair partners, new activities, excessive spending, or gambling—because he doesn't want to feel the emotions that he's feeling (lost, without purpose, bored, unhappy, depressed). So, he does everything in his power to distract himself from those negative thoughts and feelings. He's unwilling to process the emotions he is hiding from himself. Thus, he creates two separate lives.

As a spouse you are likely feeling angry and hurt. You feel unwanted, unloved, and left out. You can't believe what he is doing or how he doesn't care about you and your family. You may be thinking, "How could he do this to me?" "How can he just walk away from our marriage?" "How can he ignore the vows he made all those years ago?" "Why is he throwing our marriage away?" "Don't all those years together mean anything to him?" These are all normal thoughts. This is the time when you need to double down on self-care and work on managing your emotions. Although it seems he is doing this to *you*, he is really doing it to *himself*.

I can't stress this enough: The MLC is not about you; it's about him and his lost identity. I tell my clients to think of their husband as having brain cancer or that this husband is the MLC husband, not the one you fell in love with. Detaching from his current behavior is critical to your survival.

During this phase especially, the MLC husband feels entitled. He has provided for the family all of these years, even if you also helped to support the family or even made more money than he did. He now thinks it is his right to have a little fun. He takes up new hobbies, works out, loses weight, and finds new, younger friends. This stage is the one that is often viewed as the stereotypical MLC. While these behaviors are symptoms, they are not the cause. Unfortunately, this is the picture of MLC that the media and movies focus on.

You may also notice during the replay stage that your husband becomes very secretive. He starts lying, omitting, or telling partial truths. He may create different profiles on social media and change his relationship status. You may see him put his phone face down on the table, whereas before, he would place it face up. He might change passwords and become secretive. It's common for him to spend a long time in the car on his phone before coming into the house. He gets mad if you look over his shoulder or ask questions about who is on the phone. Prior to this phase, he might freely share his conversations and texts with you. Before he would announce, "I'm going to the store." Now, he just leaves, and if you ask where he's going, he might snap, "I'm going out!"

The MLC husband may stop wearing his wedding ring at this point, blaming it on playing sports, or working with machinery. Prior to this, those activities didn't stop him from wearing it. He hides things because he knows he is doing something wrong. He keeps his new life separate and secret. He doesn't tell his parents anything and even his old friends frequently have no idea what is going on. He doesn't tell anyone about his new life, even if he moves out and is separated from the family. There may be no mention to his parents or friends that he has an affair partner. He keeps his life compartmentalized: family life vs. MLC life.

Conversations with you, friends, colleagues, and family are on the surface, nothing deep. The kids, however, often know about his MLC life because they become included in some of his new activities. One left behind spouse told me her twenty-two-year-old daughter went out to lunch with her dad's new, younger friends who were not much older than she was. The daughter was shocked because the friends didn't even know her father had kids, let alone the fact that they were close to her age.

Replay is the time when he ramps up his affair if he is having one (and most do). Some are more secretive about it and even deny it, while others flaunt it all over social media. It all depends on the person. For the left behind spouse, this can be one of the hardest stages. I found this stage to be excruciating. Your guy, the one who maybe was also the Boy Scout-type, or who you would have described as a loving and devoted spouse, is suddenly having an affair. Of course, if he has moved out of the house, he feels an affair is ok and he's justified because you are separated, even though you are still married. It is often one of the longest stages because of the affair partner. Oftentimes, they move in together, break up, and try again. It takes time for him to figure out that she isn't the solution to his internal problem.

He often does things with the affair partner he would have never done with you, like buying spur-of-the-moment flights to new places and expensive concert tickets with her, when before he didn't want to spend any money on those things. Some have multiple affairs, bouncing from one partner to another. He pushes to leave the house so he can move in with his affair partner or into his own apartment. One of the reasons this stage is so hard is because he doesn't want a connection with you anymore. You feel like you are unimportant to him, and you don't matter to him anymore. For a time, you actually don't matter to him. But take heart, this often changes later in the crisis. The best thing you can do right now is focus on you and your happiness. Build your support team with other women going through this. We'll talk more about this in Chapter Six.

Depression

Your husband begins to feel like a failure because nothing he has done has helped him feel better about himself. The external distractions and his new life didn't solve his issues. Moving out, getting an affair partner, getting divorced, or switching jobs are all outside solutions to an inside problem.

The affair partner isn't what he thought she would be. Turns out, she's not perfect either. Some men get professional help while others stay stuck. His appearance changes again. He may go in a total opposite direction by growing his hair longer or having a shaggy beard. I saw one man in an MLC group who dyed his hair blue when it had been natural before. He starts to look older than he really is. He may look shaggy and ragged because he is not taking care of himself. Many times, you have no idea what's going on in this stage because he has moved out, and you don't see him much anymore. His affair partner may still be around, but she becomes a mere companion, someone to accompany him during outings and activities.

He may withdraw during this time, and you may barely hear from him. Although there is nothing you can do for him, you must keep working on yourself, your needs, your goals, and your future.

Withdrawal

In many cases, during this stage, he starts thinking about all of the damage he has done. He may begin to regret how he hurt you and the rest of his family. Many times, this is when the fog begins to lift, and he starts to see all that he has done. One guy on an MLC forum described it like the Claritin commercial where they peel away the blurry scene into a clear scene.

During this stage, he may remove himself from your life completely, so you may not see him at all or rarely hear from him. Depression and withdrawal often come together. He feels he doesn't deserve you and may even tell you that. Low self-esteem is a common theme around this time. Some do not make it to the acceptance stage and are in so much pain that they may die by suicide. This is a very hard phase for the standing spouse because you may feel like he's never coming back, that it's over for good. Not hearing from him for months on end can be excruciating. Do your best to persevere. Lean on your support group and remember that this is all part of MLC.

Acceptance

He may be hesitant, not knowing how you will react. He doesn't want to be rejected, and he's not sure how to reintegrate. That's when all the skills you have learned (those are coming up in future chapters) are critical to his coming home. It's easier for him to slip back in if you have left the door open for him. The left behind spouse is often the last person he reconnects with (but not always).

By now, he probably looks older, more tired. Midlife crisis is exhausting because of all of the emotional turmoil. Many men who have come through MLC appear to have aged ten years. His face may not have the same tension or anger anymore. There is more light in his eyes. If he's truly coming out of the crisis, he'll look more at ease. He may be apologetic, but oftentimes men struggle to verbalize with what happened. He may say, "I messed up," but not give any details. Or, he may say nothing. He's not sure how to come home, so he may start by hanging out with you and the family. Reconnecting with pets may be one of his first moves. He may try to act like everything is ok and hope you don't ask too many questions.

He will start engaging with you more and reconnecting with family and old friends. He's testing the waters to see if he's still accepted. He may try to make up for some of the damage he caused. Some men come back fully ready to rebuild, but for most, it takes time for them to settle in because they still struggle with emotional ups and down (one day being warm and loving, the next distant and irritable), which leads to a lot of second guessing and wavering. Some will leave and come back a few times before they are home for good. Many fear discussing the crisis because they don't want to face their guilt and your pain. In many cases, reattachment can be a slow process. Just because he's back physically doesn't mean he's fully back emotionally.

Most likely, your MLCer's homecoming will not be the grand event you might envision. He won't make an announcement that he is ready to move back in and become part of the family again. Instead, he might start spending more time at home. He may start sleeping over in the guest room or on the couch. Eventually, his time at home increases. He is still broken when he comes home, as there is still much work to do. The transition is gradual. This is when all the skills you have learned—giving him space, listening, not being his mother, not offering suggestions—are extremely important.

His return isn't the finish line; it's the starting point of a new phase. How you handle it can make a big difference in how well he reintegrates and reconnects. As throughout the entire MLC, you will need to continue to be patient and allow him to be responsible for his own healing. Meanwhile, you will have learned new skills, you will know how to stand on your own, and your happiness won't be dependent on him.

One day, he may start talking about the future with you in a positive way. He may talk about an exit strategy for retirement. You will finally hear hope in his voice. He may go overboard buying you presents, want to go on trips with you, and for the first time since it all started, won't let you out of his sight. Signs of the old husband you married are coming back are mixed in with this new guy. He starts complimenting you in front of other people. He may be in awe of everything you have done while he was gone. He may or may not talk to you about what he has been through, but don't push. Just be there as a friend. Listen to him. At this point, don't ask any questions. We'll talk more about the home coming in the last chapter.

A cautionary point on the stages

Many MLC coaches do not believe in the stages because oftentimes, the MLC spouse is all over the place and moves in and out of the stages with no rhyme or reason. I share them with you because they helped me understand the crisis better and I took comfort in the fact that MLC is so common that there are actually stages of MLC behavior.

Jennifer, a fellow standing spouse, had this insight: "Almost all of the MLCers seem to have either an avoidant or anxious attachment style and regardless of their type, a primary indicator that lends itself to MLC is the change, the big change. They used to be such good fathers and suddenly, they have no interest in doing things with the kids, or they used to give compliments all the time and now they can't even look you in the eyes. They used to talk poorly about partying and drinking, and suddenly, their only friends are bar flies."

Types of MLCers

The drastic shift in the behavior of your MLC spouse can manifest in different ways. Although every man's MLC is unique, there are some common types of MLCers that reflect how they handle the turmoil. These types help explain the patterns you might see in your husband's behavior.

The Sporadic Connector

Your husband connects with you or checks in every so often to see what you are doing. He also occasionally does things with the kids. He pops in and out from time to time. He might be absent for a few days, a few weeks, or a few months, but eventually he checks in to see what you're up to while living his MLC life separately. Most of the husbands of the women in my groups tend to be this type.

The Chaos Creator

He loves drama. He sucks you in, comes home for a bit, gets everyone excited and hopeful that he might be home for good, then leaves again. Back and forth, up and down, like a yo-yo. He gets mad at the affair partner, blows up, comes home, and then goes back to her. You may need to set some boundaries for yourself and your kids when this happens but do this with your MLC coach. It's a case-by-case situation. The best thing you can do is to try to stay out of the drama. Don't engage in his venting. Don't talk about the affair partner. His mess is his mess. Teach your kids to protect their emotions as well. Tell them: "Dad is struggling with some things, so we're going to give him some space. You can always come talk to me." Plan special outings with your kids. If your husband comes along, great; if he doesn't, don't make a big deal about it.

The Runaway

This type literally just disappears. One standing spouse thought her husband was gone for good. She never heard from him, never even knew which state he was in, but she did know he was alive. After a few years, he started contacting her. As with the other types, it's best you continue to move forward with your life.

Understanding the different types of MLCers helps you recognize how your husband's behavior might play out during his crisis. But why does this happen in the first place? What drives a man to suddenly change so drastically, abandon his sense of self, or turn into someone unrecognizable? To answer that, we will explore the underlying causes of an MLC in the next chapter.

What to Do Now

For now, there are a few important things you should do. For starters, stop scrambling emotionally and start mapping the terrain. Knowledge is power. Research and speak with other MLC spouses to learn strategies to prepare for the emotional and mental climb ahead. Download or print the MLC checklist.

Next, detach emotionally from his behavior. This is difficult, but it is necessary. Repeat to yourself daily, "This is not about me." When he lashes out or withdraws, visualize a glass wall between you. You can see him, but his chaos can't touch you.

Stay calm and kind, but don't chase or try to fix him. Recognize the signs, but don't obsess over the stages. Remember, this is his crisis, even though it affects every aspect of your life.

Finally, commit to a minimum of fifteen minutes of self-care a day. This could include taking a walk, listening to positive podcasts, meditation, journaling, or doing anything that feels good to you.

Key Takeaways

- Midlife crisis is a full-blown identity crisis, not a cliché.

- Your husband is suffering silently inside. Even if he looks selfish, reckless, or cruel, he is drowning in emotions he's never learned to process.

- Personality changes are the first warning signs. Secretive behavior, mood swings, obsessing over his phone, and withdrawing from the family are major red flags.

- There's a playbook that most MLC husbands unconsciously follow: Bomb drop, withdrawal, contradiction, distancing, etc. Once you recognize the script, you can stop taking it personally.

- The crisis may follow stages, but they aren't neat or linear.

- There are different types of MLCers. Knowing your husband's type may help you manage your expectations and your energy.

- Understanding MLC is your first step toward emotional survival. The more you understand what's happening, the less you'll blame yourself and the stronger you will become.

Chapter 3.

THE HIDDEN PAIN BEHIND
HIS MIDLIFE CRISIS

*Sometimes, the person falling apart right beside you is hiding it so
well, even you can't see the pieces.*

~ Anonymous

I sat at the kitchen table at 3 a.m., my computer in front of
me, staring off into the dark backyard, wondering how this
all happened. He was upstairs asleep (he hadn't yet moved out). As
I replayed in my mind all of the weird behaviors and conversations
over the last few months, I wondered, *was it something I said? Something
I missed? Have I not supported him enough? Am I not enough? Haven't we been
happy?* I really thought we were.

We had it all; two wonderful children, a beautiful house, and
his great job. We hosted friends and family and traveled to exotic
places. We were well on our way to a great retirement where we
could enjoy life more. So why wasn't he happy? I thought if I could
understand why he had changed so drastically I could fix it, fix us.
If I could just find the right answer I could fix everything. I had
spent hours searching through articles, watching videos, digging

into books, trying to figure out why my husband had changed so much... and how I could change him back. I was looking for an explanation, the missing piece that would snap everything back into place. What I eventually realized is that the answer wasn't hidden in some magical article or expert opinion. The real answer was this; Midlife crisis isn't logical. Nothing about it makes sense. It's emotional.

Kara Oh, author of *Male Midlife Crisis: Why It Causes Men to Destroy Their Families, Finances, and Even Commit Suicide*, explains that many men spend their entire lives suppressing any emotion that doesn't look like strength. Vulnerability is seen as failure. By the time MLC hits, they aren't just confused, they are terrified and have no idea how to talk about it. My husband's crisis wasn't something I could solve or prevent because it wasn't about me at all. Once I understood that, I finally stopped fighting to fix him and started focusing on understanding MLC and myself. That's when everything began to change.

If you're like most spouses, your first instinct is to look for a reason, anything to explain why the man you loved and trusted has seemingly vanished before your eyes. Was it something you did? Was it a slow buildup of resentment? Is there someone else, or is he losing his mind? The truth is more complicated, and far more heartbreaking. Midlife crisis isn't about you, or your marriage, or even the affair partner he might be chasing. It's about him facing demons he doesn't know exist, an internal identity crisis triggered by years, and sometimes decades, of suppressed fears, regrets, shame, and unmet dreams.

Kara Oh points out that men are conditioned from childhood to focus on achievement and strength, but not on vulnerability. They are allowed to express anger. They are allowed to express love. But fear, sadness, and shame? Those emotions are forbidden. When those feelings finally surface at midlife, they don't just feel overwhelming, they feel impossible to talk about, even to the people who know them best. So, let's dig into what really drives a man into MLC and why it often blindsides everyone, himself included. As Kara Oh explains, when a man looks back at his life during midlife, "What he sees, what he feels, is the void—the hole, the emptiness—that stems from the denial of his true feelings and emotions."[12] That emptiness terrifies him. And because he was never taught to name or process those emotions, he panics and often lashes out at the people closest to him.

Once you understand that your husband's pain runs deeper than just surface-level unhappiness, and that it's rooted in old wounds, silent pressures, and emotional habits he was never taught how to process, it becomes easier to see why an MLC can be so overwhelming and unpredictable. There isn't a singular cause for it. Instead, it's often a collision of many life experiences hitting all at once, creating a perfect emotional storm. In fact, that is how I often describe it to clients. "The perfect storm."

Dr. Bob Nguyen, author of *Midlife Crisis; Adapt, Evolve, Survive*, writes candidly about male identity struggles in midlife. In the book, he describes it this way: "We work our asses off for years, most times too busy to stop and question what lies at the end of the path."[13] Midlife crisis is a slow breakdown, one that even they don't always see coming until it hits them full force. When that happens, they appear to snap and exhibit a sudden change in behavior, which is how it feels to the left behind spouse. Let's explore some of the rocky terrain that can trigger an MLC so you can better understand what might be happening underneath the surface.

Why Is This Happening? Contributing Factors of a Midlife Crisis

There is no one cause of MLC, but there are many factors that can contribute to this identity crisis. Many are closely intertwined and it's rarely one specific thing but multiple.

Health and Mortality Awareness

Facing serious health issues can trigger a crisis, whether it is the MLCer's own health issues or that of someone they love. In my husband's case, I almost died twice due to health issues, and I believe my near-death experiences, among other things, played a role in triggering his crisis. He preferred to leave me on his own terms rather than face the fear of losing me unexpectedly due to an illness. Concerns about aging and mortality can heighten feelings of time slipping away. Death of a parent or a good friend can also trigger MLC, as well as receiving a diagnosis of a terminal illness. In my coaching practice, almost all of the husbands of the wives I coach have lost someone close recently, such as a parent or good friend, and they didn't know how to handle it.

Job and Career Challenges

Feeling stuck, undervalued, or past their peak in a career is common. Many men climb the ladder of success, reach the top, and realize their career achievements don't bring the happiness they expected. Younger colleagues feel like a threat, intensifying the feelings of inadequacy. Transitioning from high-stakes jobs, like the military, can also result in a loss of purpose, especially when camaraderie and significance are gone. They might say, "I gave twenty years to this company and now they act like I'm disposable."

Financial and Provider Pressures

Men often feel the societal burden of being the primary provider, even when their spouse contributes financially. This pressure can leave them questioning their purpose and self-worth when financial stability is achieved or threatened. This is a huge factor that they often complain about. "I'm just a paycheck to you." "I'm tired of being responsible for everyone's happiness." "I'm just here to pay the bills." I hear this from so many of my clients that I know this pressure is enormous. Looking back on my own marriage, I now realize how heavy this pressure was on my husband, and how I could have more openly expressed my gratitude for him in this area.

Unresolved Trauma or Grief

Past traumas or unresolved emotional issues often resurface during midlife, especially when they have been buried for decades. Many men were taught from an early age to suppress emotions, viewing vulnerability as a weakness. Without the tools to process their feelings, they resort to unhealthy coping mechanisms such as affairs, substance abuse, and impulsive spending. This is often a new behavior for them. The husband who never drank suddenly goes out to bars. The husband who has been faithful all of these years suddenly has an affair.

Loss of Purpose

Empty nest syndrome, career ceilings, and major life transitions can lead to questions like, "Is this all there is?" or "What's my legacy?" Without a clear purpose in life, men tend to feel as if they have lost their compass in life. They might feel bored, stuck, and unhappy. I have heard many wives mention their husbands say they feel disconnected. Mine said that as well.

Perceived Lack of Happiness

Many men go searching for happiness, believing it lies in external changes—new relationships, fast or fancy cars, or expensive purchases—only to find these only provide temporary distractions. One wife shared with me that her husband admitted, "I don't remember the last time I was happy." This illustrates how dissatisfaction often originates from within, not from their external circumstances or from you, the spouse.

Unmet Expectations in Relationships

Over time, couples can unconsciously expect their partner to provide happiness. When men feel they can't fix their wives' unhappiness—or their own—they may withdraw or rebel, believing the marriage itself is the problem. Ultimately, both partners are responsible for their individual happiness, but this realization often comes too late.

These are just some of the contributing factors for MLC. Which of these factors come into play for your husband, or whether another factor is present, all depends on your husband's personality and how he handles various factors within his own life. Some men are able to handle life's challenges and changes better than others. After talking to other left behind spouses, I have found that much of the cause of MLC can be attributed to the perceived lack of happiness the MLC spouse feels.

When you're single, you know you're 100 percent responsible for your own happiness. Then, when you start dating and get married, your partner adds to your happiness, and it feels like you're on cloud nine; you feel like you're at 110 percent. But as the relationship grows and deepens, your spouse may begin to expect you to keep supplying that extra happiness. Over time, he might even start blaming you when he is unhappy, shifting the responsibility for his joy onto your shoulders instead of his own. He goes searching for happiness only to find that it's not something to be found outside of himself, it's something within. External solutions, such as moving out, having an affair, going on lavish trips, or buying a sports car, do not provide intrinsic value. True fulfillment comes from rediscovering one's passion and purpose, focusing on the positives in life, and giving back to others and community.

So, while one potential path out is for your husband to rediscover his own passion and purpose, that's something *he* must find for himself. As his wife, you can support him by giving him time and space to do that. Maybe that looks like encouraging his ideas, even the ones that seem a little crazy. But it's not your job to lead him there. Ideally, this happens before MLC occurs, but the fact that so many men experience MLC is a testament that it is difficult to break out of one's comfort zone until a crisis hits. "Often though, it takes a crisis for us to reassess where we are and how to move forward," Nguyen notes.[14] And that is what the MLC is all about; it is a form of depression.

When Midlife Crisis Hides Deeper Pain

What's happening to your husband may look like reckless and crazy behavior on the outside (the impulsivity, the anger, the monstering, the distance) but underneath it all, there's often something more going on: depression.

It's not the depression you might expect. This type of depression often goes underdiagnosed because the more traditional symptoms of clinical depression like sadness and crying, don't show. Instead, his depression behavior might look like quitting his job, chasing an affair partner, or pulling away from everyone he loves. In men, depression often hides behind anger, withdrawal, escapism, and denial. He may not even recognize that he is depressed. In his mind, he's just irritated by everything and everyone. He's blaming work, circumstances, or "stupid people" without realizing it's coming from within. He appears to be stuck in a perpetually bad mood. You can't diagnose him. You can't rescue him. You can't explain it away. (Believe me I tried.) However, knowing that depression is a hidden part of this can help stop you from personalizing his behavior. You feel like you aren't enough, but the truth is, he feels like he's not enough and he doesn't know how to deal with it.

As much as you want to help him, it's best not to tell him you suspect he's depressed. He doesn't want any help from you right now. Understanding this can give you more perspective and can help you find your way back to yourself while you leave him alone to fight his own inner battles. This might seem counterintuitive to your natural urge to love him back to who he was or to help him talk it out. But at this stage, doing that with your husband will only push him further away. The best thing to do is to give him space. Practice active listening if he does talk. Most importantly, leave him alone and let him figure it out. Because he is at war with himself, he can't receive your love the way he used to. So, he begins to grasp for something, anything outside of himself just to feel better, because all he wants is to feel better.

The Illusion of External Happiness

In a desperate attempt to fix the internal emptiness they don't understand, many men in MLC go searching for happiness in all the wrong places. This seems logical since we are all socialized to believe that our happiness comes from external sources.

Advertising messages exaggerate and capitalize on this. We are inundated with messages about how anti-aging products, luxury cars, and over-priced clothing can make us look and feel younger, be happier, and avoid any perceived negative effects of life. Subconsciously, we are lulled into believing that these external solutions are the keys to happiness. Years and years of this media bombardment convince us that this is true. So, we get the job, the house, the car, the spouse, the kids, and all of that is supposed to make us happy. But if happiness is absent internally, then we can never be truly happy.

This is where MLC and depression intersect. When men reach midlife and realize that all of the external markers of success haven't brought them lasting happiness, they may panic. They assume that something external must be missing, so they seek to change careers, buy a sports car, or leave their marriage in search of excitement. But the reality is, it's the thoughts he has about himself that have everything to do with his happiness.

Happiness is a mindset and not a product of external factors. Happiness and fulfillment are internal, not external. So, if a man feels unfulfilled or perceives that his wife doesn't admire him anymore, he may believe that changing external factors will restore his sense of self-worth. But until he addresses his emotional needs, no amount of excitement or change will provide him lasting satisfaction.

The "Upper Limit Problem" and How It Relates to Midlife Crisis

While reading *The Big Leap* by Gay Hendricks, I realized that in addition to these contributing factors for MLC, the "Upper Limit Problem" could very well play a role in an MLC, especially when it comes to what Hendericks calls "subconscious self-sabotage." Based on Hendricks's ideas, here are a few things your MLC husband might be going through. See if you recognize any of them. I certainly did with my husband.

Hitting a Ceiling of Success or Happiness

By the time they reach midlife, many men have checked off all of the boxes: successful career, family life, and financial stability. One would think they would be proud and satisfied with their achievements. From the outside, it looks like they have it all, but what's happening on the inside could be a very different story.

Deep down, issues start bubbling up. He may start to wonder, "is this all there is?" or "Don't I deserve to be happier than this?" This discomfort can leave him feeling unsettled, confused, and often overwhelmed. And because he doesn't know how to process these emotions, he unconsciously creates chaos to escape the thoughts or to sabotage his current life circumstances. He feels trapped by it all and withdraws emotionally, then may turn to an affair, quit his job, or even walk away from a long-term marriage. He might abandon his marriage because he associates it with the old version of himself that felt stuck. It's heartbreaking to hear clients, some who have been married more than thirty years, explain that their husband just walked away with no warning and no real explanation.

The Hidden Beliefs That Sabotage Happiness

In his book, *The Big Leap,* Hendricks talks about the hidden beliefs that pop up when someone hits a certain level of success. If unaddressed, these beliefs can sabotage happiness. Brooke Castillo's work also backs this up perfectly. Castillo teaches that the thoughts we have, the little sentences running through our brains all-day, are usually just stories we tell ourselves. They are not facts. They are thoughts we have picked up from childhood, our parents, and society, that we have accepted without ever questioning them. These thoughts become automatic. Over time, they carve deep grooves in our mind, like ruts in a road. The beliefs that Hendrick describes are actually these unchallenged thoughts playing on repeat, stuck in those grooves. Some might include:

- **I'm fundamentally flawed.** Somewhere along the way, your husband may have learned to believe he wasn't enough, that success had been a fluke, not something he truly earned. Down deep he might think, *I've been fooling everyone; I don't deserve this level of success.* Engaging in an affair, a divorce, or reckless behavior creates real life failures that prove this belief to him. These actions become a self-fulfilling prophecy. My husband didn't believe he deserved the level of success he had earned. I never understood why because he's brilliant.

- **Success will isolate me.** Maybe your husband grew up believing if he got "too big" he would lose the people he loves. So, when he succeeds, he feels lonely, as if he no longer belongs. He might start to feel like he's outgrowing the people around him—family, friends, even you—and that can trigger panic. Instead of feeling proud, he feels disconnected, so he runs from it.

- **Happiness and success come at a cost.** He might think that life always requires a painful trade-off, that if things are too good, something bad has to happen. Somewhere deep inside, he might believe he can't have it all. Therefore, to keep his success, he has to sacrifice something else, like his marriage or his personal happiness.

None of these beliefs are facts, they're just deeply ingrained thoughts that he never stopped to question. You may have similar beliefs as well. Beliefs are just thoughts that we have thought over and over until they solidify into a belief. When negative beliefs go unchecked, they can create feelings of fear, shame, guilt, and loneliness, which drive actions like withdrawal, relationship sabotage, or chasing excitement outside the marriage. As Castillo often says, "Circumstances don't cause our feelings, our thoughts do." So, when everything looks good enough, stability can feel terrifying. If your husband is accustomed to chaos, then success and stability might actually feel unsafe to him, like something bad is right around the corner. Instead of leaning into a happy, settled life, he unconsciously tries to reset things through conflict or drama, like having an affair or quitting his job. Of course, this behavioral response is not logical. But to a scared brain stuck in old beliefs, chaos feels safer than peace.

Projection of Discontent

One of the hardest things to deal with during your husband's MLC is how often he blames you for his unhappiness. Instead of recognizing that his dissatisfaction is coming from himself, he projects it onto you, finds fault with your marriage, his career, the kids, anything besides himself. He often will make up things or rewrite history just to be able to blame you. You are the problem in his mind because he can't face the real problem inside of him.

This is why you can't take his words and actions personally, even when they cut deep and are so brutal. His anger, accusations, and withdrawal are not about you. They are driven by his inner struggles. This is probably one of the hardest points to get across to my clients, so please hear me on this. His monstering is not about you; it's about his unhappiness.

Why the "Why" Won't Save You

So, what does all this mean? The important thing to remember is that you may never know the why behind your husband's MLC, you just know the impact. I know you think knowing the why will make you feel better, but it won't. You can't control your spouse's behaviors or choices; you can only control yourself and how you respond to him.

In the beginning of my husband's MLC, I was so obsessed with the why because I thought I was the reason for his unhappiness. Over time, I realized that it didn't even matter why he went into MLC. The bottom line is that it happened. How I chose to deal with it and move forward with my life is all that mattered to me.

One standing spouse said, "I think we left behind spouses all try to figure out the mystery, to find a reason or an answer to why this happened or explain their actions and way of thinking. Their choices and logic don't add up, so we try and try to figure out the riddle. But I think oftentimes, things just don't add up. There is no logic. And that's why it's MLC, because it doesn't make sense." She continued, "Having conversations with my husband after the crisis [who is now home], I can see he doesn't even know why he did some of the things he did. A lot of it sounds like desperation. What he thought was best for him at the time of despair and hopelessness.

We [as left behind spouses] are not insane, but we nearly go insane trying to figure it out. You cannot. It's not for you to figure out."

As this spouse shares, often men in MLC don't even remember what they did during their own MLC. This is extremely common. It's as if they are in a trance. Some don't even remember having an affair. When looking at pictures, some believe they spent holidays and vacations with their families, but they weren't actually present for those events. It sounds weird, but the brain blocks out much of this time in their lives.

Although you may never know the exact cause of your husband's MLC, being aware of the stages, types, and contributing factors can help you understand.

Here are a few important takeaways to keep in mind:

- **It's not about you.** Your husband's actions are not a reflection of your value or the quality of your marriage. The MLC is often his reaction to his internal conflict.

- **Self-sabotage can be destructive.** Recognizing the signs can help you detach emotionally from the muck and the chaos. You are not to blame.

- **Explore what makes you happy.** Just as your husband is responsible for his happiness, you are responsible for your own happiness.

Instead of waiting for him to snap out of it, focus on thriving in your own life.

As a left behind spouse, you may feel you have lost your purpose when your husband moves out. You may feel you have lost your identity as a wife. Due to the tremendous grief when your husband is gone or unhappy, you might also lose your passion and zest for life. You go through a grieving period similar to experiencing the death of a spouse. In reality, it is the death of a marriage, at least the marriage you once knew. But it's how you handle this that matters now.

As you manage this difficult time, you have many questions and probably few answers. That is all perfectly normal. One common question that standing spouses have is, "How long does the MLC last?" Everyone is different, so it depends on the individual. Most sources say an MLC can last anywhere from three to seven years. That's a long time, and much of it depends on how long your husband is with the affair partner, whether he gets help, and how long it takes him to come out of the depression. In the meantime, remember that none of this is your fault, no matter what state your marriage was in prior to your husband's MLC. As you allow him to work on his emotional issues, you do the same. Focus on you and your mental and emotional health. Later on, you will find suggestions and resources to help you cope during this time, however long it lasts.

Another common question is, "How do I survive this?" You can't make his MLC go faster, and it's futile to try. Unfortunately, you can make it worse. There are two paths to surviving his MLC: 1) you can push him away so that he never comes back, or 2) you can let him figure this out on his own. Be there and be a friend when he finds his way back. If you do "force" him out of it he will go through the crisis again until he really figures himself out. It's best to leave him alone. It's not your job to drag him up the mountain. It's your job to keep climbing for yourself. Instead of waiting for him to snap out of it, focus on thriving in your own life. What have you always wanted to do but put off? Whether it's a new hobby, career goal, or simply finding joy in small moments, this is your chance to reclaim yourself.

You want things to move along at a speedy pace, but as hard as it is, you have to live your life without him and move forward. The best advice I ever received was, "Pretend he's dead. How would you live your life if he were dead?" As harsh as that advice sounds, it was very helpful. The truth is, it really does feel like your husband is dead when he moves out of the house. However, when he comes around, you be you. Be kind and give him the unconditional love you have always offered him, but within the safe boundaries you have set for yourself. It's a bit like having your left foot on the brake and your right foot on the gas pedal at the same time. You hold space for him, but you live your life.

If he moves out, it's often easier on you. Although you may be lonely, you are not subjected to his horrible moods, tantrums, or bad behavior. You don't keep track of his coming and going. You can gather yourself and find your peace, on your own, in your house and your life. But just because he moves out, doesn't mean he won't pop in and out. That happens quite frequently. When it does, the best thing to do is just go with the flow. If you keep the door open, it's easier for him to return when he has emerged from his crisis. In Chapter 12, I cover several tips to handle accepting him back into your home.

I'm not saying that you should ask him to leave. That decision needs to come from him. But if he chooses to move out, and many do, you can allow it without falling apart. You might say, "This isn't what I want, but I respect your decision. If you feel this will make you happy, I won't stop you."

Most MLCers do move out during the crisis; however, those who stay often create a living hell for the standing spouse and the family. Many standing spouses whose husbands remained at home have shared with me that they just try to keep their head down, stay busy in their own activities, and try not to engage in combative behavior. If he does stay, give him space to do his own thing. Don't be controlling or ask questions about his whereabouts. Make sure you have your own safe space where you can gather your thoughts. Be sure to take good care of yourself during this time. If you don't like what's going on at home, going for a walk helps tremendously to clear your head. Make plans with your friends and family. Live your life. Here are a few ideas to start now.

The Five Most Effective Actions During a Midlife Crisis

1. **Anchor yourself in self-care.** Prioritize your physical and mental health with activities like walking, journaling, or listening to uplifting podcasts. Your well-being is nonnegotiable.

2. **Release the "Why" and focus on "What Now."** Stop obsessing over the reasons behind his behavior and focus on creating a plan for yourself.

3. **Set boundaries without closing the door:** Protect yourself from unnecessary drama but stay kind and open to communication when he reaches out.

4. **Rediscover your own happiness.** Make a list of things that bring you joy and start doing them. That might include picking up an old hobby, spending time with friends, or pursuing a dream.

5. **Cultivate compassion while staying strong.** Remember, this is his crisis, not yours. You can show empathy without enabling bad behavior.

What to Do Now

As harsh as this might sound, it's helpful: Pretend he's dead. What would you do if your husband was dead? Seek your purpose. Figure out how to create your own happiness without him. Focus on your life, the activities you love, have longed to do, or are curious about. When he interacts with you, be nice, be kind, and listen. Avoid heated discussions. Don't be controlling and don't ask him questions.

Make a list of things that make you happy and fill your mind throughout the day with positive messages, such as certain songs, conversations or activities with positive friends, or uplifting podcasts. For podcasts, I love "The Life Coach Podcast" by Brooke Castillo, "Weight Loss Made Real" by Cookie Rosenblum, and because I'm an entrepreneur, Jan Ditchfield's "The Business of Good." Find what appeals to you. Make a ritual of this sacred time for yourself, make it a habit, so that you look forward to it.

Another activity that will absolutely help you through this time is to prioritize your physical well-being. Fit exercise into your regular routine. Movement releases stress and allows you to focus on yourself instead of on your husband's behavior.

Key Takeaways

- Midlife crisis often feels unpredictable, but many men follow a surprisingly similar script.
- You may not understand why this is happening but know it's not your fault.
- Focus on thriving in your own life rather than waiting for him to snap out of it. It is a marathon, not a sprint.
- It's crucial to build resilience and set boundaries for your emotional well-being.
- Many things can contribute to or trigger an MLC, but it really doesn't matter why. What matters is how you respond to it.

Chapter 4.

STRENGTHENING YOUR CORE: IT'S NOT ABOUT YOU, BUT IT'S ALL UP TO YOU

You won't always know where the path leads. Just focus on the next brave step.

~ Anonymous

In the days after my husband moved out, I didn't even want to get out of bed. His leaving felt like the end of everything I had known. It was a death. I was devastated.

I had no motivation for anything. I didn't want to get dressed, take a shower, or work on my blog. I didn't feel like cooking. I didn't feel like eating. I didn't want to talk to anyone. I didn't want to do anything except cry and curl up in a ball on the bathroom floor. I was a complete mess. I was so alone. I felt no one understood me. Looking back, I see that it wasn't an end, it was the beginning of a long journey back to myself. I didn't know where this painful path would lead me. What I did realize is that every journey starts with a first step, even if that step is just surviving the next few minutes or making it through one more hard day.

If this feels familiar—feeling alone, overwhelmed, and just trying to hang on—please know, it's ok. You're allowed to feel like you're barely clinging to the side of the mountain. Those feelings are normal when you face something this steep, this rugged. I'm here to tell you that you will make it. Every climber hits brutal patches where the rock crumbles and the path disappears. When you're the spouse left behind by an MLC in a long-term marriage, this stretch of the climb is especially brutal. It will test your strength, your spirit, and your will to keep going. So, give yourself some grace. You are scaling one of the hardest mountains life can put before you. It's ok to rest, to cry, to scream, and to catch your breath. In so many ways, this is much harder than death because you're living in the in-between.

Managing as a left behind spouse through MLC is excruciating and probably one of marriage's hardest journeys. It's certainly the hardest one I've ever faced. I wish I could reach through this page and wrap you in a big hug right now and whisper that it's going to be ok and that you are not alone. Because it will be ok, somewhere further along the climb. You may feel like you will never get there, but you will. It just takes time. Lots of time... and lots of courage. Once you reach the summit, the view is beautiful, and you finally feel like you can breathe freely again. But guess what? You have already taken the first step. You're here, you're figuring this out. It just takes one step at a time. Those first steps are powerful, even though they don't always *feel* powerful. Some days, you feel stuck in the same painful loop, living the same day over and over, like the movie *Ground Hog Day*.

It's easy to feel hopeless, but that's not who you are. Deep inside, there's a whisper, a part of you that knows your potential and gently reminds you that you were made for more than this moment, you were meant for bigger things. Ignoring that voice disconnects you from yourself, and it's exhausting, which is why self-care and focusing on your goals are so critical during this time. Reconnecting with yourself, even in small, simple ways, helps you move from survival mode back into the driver's seat of your life.

Rebuilding your life isn't only about what you do on the outside, it's about how you manage what's happening on the inside: your mind. As you find small ways to reconnect with yourself, you must understand that this process is difficult, not because you are broken, but because your brain is trying to protect you in the only way it knows how. Let's talk about what's really going on inside, and how you can start working with yourself instead of feeling stuck.

The Struggle Between Your Survival Brain and Your Evolved Brain

Think of your brain as the map and compass for this journey. Your survival brain clings to the old familiar trail, even if it leads you in endless circles. It's trying to keep you safe, but it's also keeping you stuck within the pain. It wants you to make a decision, to fix your marriage now or leave. Meanwhile, your evolved brain, your prefrontal cortex, is like the GPS quietly recalculating your route. It sees there is a better path forward, one that leads to growth and fulfillment. Learning to listen to the evolved part of your brain is like finding a guide to help you navigate the twists and turns ahead.

> *Blaming your husband's midlife crisis for your unhappiness is an external solution for whatever internal crisis you are experiencing.*

Once you realize your husband is in an MLC, and you realize that it's not your fault, everything starts to make more sense. Kara Oh puts it into perspective: "It is important that you not blame yourself. It has nothing to do with you. You have not failed [your husband]. If anything, you have seen that there was more to him, and you tried your best to assist him in allowing it to show itself. But he was too afraid to be that vulnerable. Being alone was easier, safer, and more familiar."[15]

Your husband's MLC is his journey, not yours, although it does impact you and your family. He's trying to figure out who he is, and he's taking the long, winding road. But it's also a parallel path. While he's on his path, you are on yours. Your journey isn't about waiting for him to come back; it's about discovering who you are when everything you've known feels like it's been turned upside down. It's about rebuilding your foundation.

Midlife crises are a classic example of someone trying to solve internal problems with external solutions. He's unhappy with his life, so he moves out, gets a girlfriend, or buys a new car, thinking it will fix everything, but it won't because those are external solutions to internal problems. Here's the hard truth for your journey: You may also be doing the same thing. Blaming your husband's MLC for your unhappiness is an external solution for whatever internal crisis you are experiencing. True happiness comes from within, not from fixing him, the marriage, or your circumstances. Imagine that you were 100 percent happy and satisfied with your inner self, the person you are, independent of your husband and your marriage. In this case, separating yourself from your husband's inner turmoil, and not blaming yourself for his actions, would likely be much easier for you. This is not to say that it would be easy to witness his behaviors during MLC, only that your stability as an individual would serve as a solid foundation to help you endure the MLC and make decisions that are best for you. So, let's get you there.

Letting go of what you can't control is one of the hardest parts of this journey. It's like climbing a mountain. You can't carry the weight of blame, resentment, or what ifs with you if you want to reach the summit. At some point, you will have to drop all of that and trust that you have everything you need within yourself to keep moving forward. This is even harder to do because your survival brain loves to resist. It's constantly scanning for danger and wants to keep you safe by holding on to what's familiar, even if it's painful. But your prefrontal cortex, the evolved part of your brain, knows better. It's the part of you that can dream big, take risks, and create a new future. The key is to stop blaming yourself for how you feel and start working *with* your brain instead of *against* it. Once you understand that these conflicting drives are just how your brain is wired, it becomes easier to focus on what you can control: your own growth and happiness.

Feeling stuck is a normal part of the journey. It's like getting lost in the woods. You feel like you're going in circles, and every direction looks the same. But being stuck isn't permanent. Once you reconnect with that part of yourself that's whispering for more, you'll find your way back to the path of growth. Every step forward, no matter how tiny, is part of the process of moving out of survival mode and into a place where you can thrive. When those quiet whispers of opportunity grow louder, be ready to lean in. For me, that moment came when one of the women's groups I belonged to, eWomenNetwork, hosted a virtual summit a few months after my husband moved out. It was a three-day event, and at the end they offered a chance to join an exclusive mastermind with the organization's founder, Sandra Yancey. That whisper grew to a roar, and I decided to go for it, thinking maybe it would kickstart my motivation for working on my business again. It helped a lot, mainly because I was required to complete projects in a timely manner. It forced me to concentrate on something besides my husband and our marriage, something that was just for me. I needed to move forward with my life because I knew the MLC would take time to progress.

Many left behind spouses hope their husband will go through the MLC quickly and be the A-plus student, but nope, not my husband. Odds are your husband won't either. Living through MLC feels excruciatingly slow. It takes more time than you realize. To survive this journey, you have to let go of "when," as in, when is he coming home? Just about the time you have given up for good, could be the time when your husband finally decides to come home. No matter how long it takes him to get through it, your responsibility is for your own happiness. Yes, you and your family are casualties of his crisis, but you cannot play the victim forever. Allow yourself to grieve, throw a pity party whenever you need to, cry, scream, yell, and get it out (in private). Then, move forward. Grieving is natural, but growth comes from shifting focus to personal goals. Coping gets easier after a while. You will still have your moments and days of grief and anger, but eventually those emotions will emerge less frequently once you realize it's up to you to create the life you really want—with or without your husband.

As you grieve and begin to take steps toward creating the life you truly want, you may find yourself standing at a crossroads, not only choosing how to heal, but also how to move forward in a way that aligns with your values and your hopes for the future.

Standing and What It Means: Choosing the Path That's Right for You

Making the decision to stand for your marriage in the face of an MLC is often misunderstood. Many people assume it's easier to stand than to walk away, but those who choose to stand know it takes immense strength and resilience. Standing for your marriage is not about being passive or refusing to move on, it's about holding space for your spouse while continuing to grow and build your own life. Standing doesn't mean you are a doormat; it means you are moving forward with your life, and you get to decide what that looks like.

As left behind spouses, most of us feel frustrated by the lack of understanding from friends, neighbors, and even therapists. The common advice is to leave and start fresh, as though walking away is the only healthy option. Yet, for those who've been in long-term marriages, the bond they share isn't something they want to abandon. Unfortunately, some therapists lack an understanding of the unique dynamics of an MLC. Many left behind spouses find it upsetting that standing for their marriage is seen as outdated or weak, especially when they know in their heart it's the right thing to do. They know something is really wrong with their husband. It's hard to explain to someone who hasn't been there, but you just know it deep in your bones. I've talked to other spouses who feel this exact way. They report hearing advice to move on, which only adds to their emotional burden. This sentiment, that standing is somehow unhealthy, can feel isolating. Yet, there are countless stories of husbands who eventually return, often regretful, and try to reconcile the damage caused during their MLC and go on to have stronger marriages.

One key insight from those who stand for their marriages is the idea of unconditional love. It's often compared to parenting: just as you wouldn't abandon your child when they're struggling and making poor choices, you don't walk away from a decades-long marriage without trying to understand and support your spouse through their struggles. We often think of unconditional love as something parents give to their children, even when parents don't approve of their kids' choices. If they screw up, get into trouble, or lose their way, you don't leave them. Wouldn't you want to extend that same grace to your husband? While you may not condone his behavior, you can still choose to stand for your marriage.

This isn't about ignoring his actions or dismissing your own needs, it's about deciding what commitment and love mean to you, even when your spouse is struggling. Just because he has given up for a time doesn't mean you have to give up too. Author Bob Proctor often references Rev. Michael Foss's work, stating, "Commitment is easy, but living into it is hard. Commitment is one of those realities that doesn't take hold until it is difficult. Commitment is deciding that the price is worth paying for the goal that will be achieved."

Getting married is easy, but living into its commitment and staying married is hard.

If you choose to stand, it's crucial to let go of blame and resentment. Try setting aside thoughts like, "It's not fair" or "He did this to me." Instead treat your spouse with kindness and compassion while you pursue your own goals; you may find a path to healing. Although there are no guarantees, numerous examples from MLC communities and personal stories reveal that reconnection is possible. For some left behind spouses, even after a divorce is finalized, they continue to hold on to hope because the emotional connection with their MLC spouse remains. They see glimpses of their spouse trying to stay connected through calls, visits, or family interactions. These actions are a clear cry for help, a desire of the MLCer to reconnect to what they still view as a solid foundation in the midst of the uncertainty of their life. Holding space doesn't mean putting your life on hold, it means continuing to move forward while allowing the possibility for your spouse to heal and find their way back.

Standing for your marriage is not about being passive or refusing to move on, it's about holding space for your spouse while continuing to grow and build your own life.

Standing doesn't mean stagnation or being stuck. Standing for your marriage means choosing long-term growth over short-term discomfort. It means being willing to experience uncertainty now because you believe in the bigger, long-term picture. Just like your husband has to learn that external solutions won't bring him happiness, you also need to learn that happiness comes from within, and that ending your marriage won't end the pain you feel, nor will it make you happy. The growth and self-discovery you experience during this time will carry you forward, no matter what happens in your marriage.

Standing also doesn't make you a doormat or mean you're standing still. It means you're choosing a path—a journey toward healing and self-discovery. It's about moving forward with your life, even as you hold space for your husband to find his way back. As you stand for your marriage, you also stand for yourself, your needs, your joy, your interests, and your well-being. How you do this is up to you, and you will find your way when you remain committed to yourself. Although you might not feel like a warrior in the beginning, you will develop a strength of character and a love of self when you remember that your husband's problems belong to him, and your growth is up to you.

You have a choice in how you deal with your husband's MLC. Some women, understandably overwhelmed and unsure about MLC, choose to file for divorce and move on, and that's always an option. But what if you knew your husband was coming back for sure? Would you want the end of your marriage to be on you? Granted, in the moment you don't know what your husband will choose to do. Your actions should not be determined by what he may or may not do. After all, he is in an abnormal, confused, and unusual state right now. Therefore, choosing to stand should be a decision you make because you believe it is the right decision for you.

Standing doesn't mean being stuck in the past or living in denial. It means continuing to move forward with your own life and goals while holding space for your husband's journey. Holding space isn't about pausing your life, it's an intentional act of hope and resilience. Some may view having hope for your husband's return as being stuck or taking the easy way out by not deciding right away what is best. But you are deciding what is best. You are deciding to stand. Standing is far from easy. It takes courage, especially in a world where divorce is common and fighting for a marriage is often dismissed. Standing takes strength and a deep commitment to your values.

In the beginning, I felt a sense of shame and embarrassment, assuming my husband's decision to leave was a reflection of our marriage. *What did I do wrong?* I believed my husband's decision to leave was a reflection of my failures as a wife, a partner, maybe even a person. I dreaded running into anyone I knew, afraid they would ask questions I couldn't answer or look at me with pity. There were whispers among neighbors, with some saying, "She should move on," as if healing had an expiration date. All of this was happening just weeks after he moved out. It felt like my entire word was unraveling and I was the only one left to explain it.

Hearing comments like, "You should leave him. You deserve better. You need to move on," was frustrating. Some even suggested I didn't believe I had other options, which wasn't true. These remarks upset me because they didn't recognize the steps I was already taking to move forward. I decided to leave the state and start a new chapter in my life on my own, without my husband. Over time, I let go of worrying about what others thought. As my youngest son put it, "Who cares what they think, Mom? If you believe he's coming back, that's what matters." Wise words, indeed.

One standing spouse told me, "It's easier to throw away what's broken than to fix it. In the case of standing spouses, we're giving our husbands the space to fix what's broken. Throw away culture is easier to digest. This is the generation that thinks unconditional love is foolish. If we hurt emotionally, we're told to put a stop to it immediately. That's how we define strong women today. But there are so many lessons to be learned from pain. I know I've learned things I wouldn't have otherwise." Her husband returned home, and now, she describes their marriage as stronger than ever.

Giving someone time and space often allow the person in crisis to sort through their confusion without added pressure. Though some individuals in an MLC may push for divorce, believing it will resolve their struggles, interestingly, many couples who divorce during MLC end up remarrying each other. This often happens because the bond remains intact, even through the hardship. I've spoken with people who remarried their ex-spouse and built a stronger relationship afterward. Others have shared similar stories about family members who reunited after divorce. For example, my hairdresser told me about her grandparents, who divorced for a few years before remarrying each other. Her grandmother referred to his MLC as "his sabbatical" and jokingly called his affair partner, "The Puta." Remarriage after divorce is more common than most realize, though it's not widely discussed. Often, when a husband returns, the couple may relocate and start fresh, which makes the stories less visible to others.

Why I Chose to Stand for My Marriage

The reason I chose to stand for my marriage is because I knew something was majorly wrong with my husband. I knew the behavior he was exhibiting wasn't him and that he tried his best to figure it out before moving out. He didn't want to leave his family, but he was unhappy with his life. He knew it wasn't me; he even told his mother that. I also chose to stand for our kids. I wanted to set a good example for them, especially my oldest son who was getting married. I wanted him to see that marriage is a long-term commitment. Times can be tough, but that doesn't mean you give up on the ones you love. Finally, I stayed because I knew in my heart it was the right thing to do. Throughout my husband's MLC, I consistently had a feeling, deep down, that I couldn't explain—a feeling that guided me to stay. I've talked to other left behind spouses who stay, and they express a similar feeling.

After you have spent some time alone and really sit with your emotions and your situation, if you don't feel a strong sense that standing for your marriage is right for you, then don't. My decision to stand isn't the only right path. I would never place the burden of shame or guilt on you for choosing differently, just as I had to learn not to carry the shame others tried to put on me for standing. Each person has the right and responsibility to make their own informed decision about their marriage during an MLC. The truth is some days you'll feel like standing while other days you won't. That's ok. That's normal. You will waver at times. We all do. You don't have to have it all figured out to keep going. Just take the next step, one day at a time. Sometimes, hearing someone else's story can remind you that there is hope, even when the trail disappears into the thick fog and you can't see more than a few steps ahead.

Sometimes, it helps to hear from someone who's walked through the same fog and made it to the other side. My friend Grace's husband is now home, and their journey through MLC has brought them closer. She shared how she knew there was something deeply wrong with him, like he was a traveler lost in a dense fog. She decided to stand by him, to walk beside him even when the path was unclear. Together, they've navigated the twists and turns, and now they're finding their way back to solid ground. Here's what she said about their experience:

> "I knew there was something deeply wrong with him. We've been together longer than we've been apart at this point. Because I believe that I know who he is, that I knew this isn't him. The love is still there. I knew if I didn't stick around, he would probably never recover from this. The loss of me and his kids. He said he kept sticking around and fighting because he knew I was [fighting] too. If I had left or wanted to move on, he said things probably would've been really destructive for him. Because the grounding was gone. My children? The life I had envisioned? I wanted to keep that intact. We didn't have a terrible life. It was a great life and marriage. I didn't want the kids to be in a single-parent home, without a father, because if I

didn't help him through this, they very well may not have a father.

My temperament also contributed to my staying. I wasn't bitter or angry. Maybe if I was, I wouldn't have been able to stay. I knew his issues were too big and later realized the affair partner was just a means to money. His biggest issue was the business, debt, and mental breakdown. The affair partner probably could have been anyone. I think knowing that also helped me stay. He even said his biggest struggle was financial and not wanting his family to be chased by creditors or anyone else, so he stayed away.

He also shared that during that time it was like an out-of-body experience. Like he was just floating, lost, aimlessly roaming. He physically felt sick and confused, couldn't sleep well, and drove around with nowhere to go. He said I was right when I said he looked soulless and empty during that time. He wanted to find a way out, but he didn't know how.

Slowly more interactions between us helped. The more he was with us the more he realized that the other life wasn't for him. We were together for long weekends and short trips here or there. Eventually, he realized the financials weren't going to change and the right thing to do was to cut his losses. He said the more he tried to fix and maintain the business the worse it would get. With every turn, the MLC tunnel started getting darker and darker while away from his family."

Grace was the glue that held her family together. Her marriage was healed, due in large part to her compassion, her willingness to gently invite her husband back into family life without pressure, and her ability to stay grounded during the chaos. She didn't chase him, but she also didn't close the door. She didn't force his healing, but she made it possible. She created a safe place for him to find his way back when he was finally ready. Hearing her describe their journey reminded me that whether children are still living at home, or are grown with families of their own, MLC can leave a lasting impact.

How Midlife Crisis and Divorce Affect Children

When deciding whether to stand for your marriage, it's important to consider the impact on your children, even if they're already in high school or are young adults just starting out on their own. I have often heard people say, "We'll just wait and get divorced after our child graduates from high school." As if delaying the decision somehow cushions the blow. However, research shows that divorce during adolescence or early adulthood can still have significant and long-lasting effects.

One study published in World Psychiatry found that children of divorced parents are at significantly higher risk for emotional and behavioral struggles, including increased risk-taking and long-term family instability.[16] Another long-term study supports the idea that the emotional effects of divorce ripple long after the actual event, and aren't magically avoided just because the child is a legal adult. Researchers found that "Those who experienced parental divorce exhibited a significantly higher risk for depression as well as lower levels of family solidarity during midlife and older ages, compared to those children whose parents' marriage was intact throughout their childhood and adult lives."[17]

Because midlife crises tend to surface around the time kids are in junior high, high school, or just entering adulthood, a crucial time when they are discovering themselves, the emotional fallout can be especially intense. These are pivotal years when children are figuring out who they are and building their sense of stability for life. They are often experiencing their own transitions, leaving home, starting a career, or beginning their own family, at the same time their parents are separating. This overlap of life changes can make it harder for them to process and accept the divorce. Adult children may struggle with the loss of family stability, especially if they still rely on their parents for emotional or financial support. Divorce at this stage doesn't just disrupt routines; it can shake the foundation they are trying to build on.

Research also highlights some common misconceptions, like the idea that children are naturally resilient or unaffected in the long run. In a book titled *The Unexpected Legacy of Divorce: A 25-Year Landmark Study*, Judith Wallerstein and her team found that many children of divorce carry fears about trust, love, and commitment well into adulthood, shaped by their parents' example. These children may develop a more cautious or skeptical view of long-term relationships.

Ultimately, midlife divorce doesn't only affect the couple, it also sends ripples through the entire family, often leaving adult children grappling with their own sense of stability and trust in relationships. According to Wallerstein's study, adult children of midlife or "gray" divorces often face additional burdens, including:

- **Family instability**: A profound sense of loss as the family structure they've always known dissolves.

- **Role reversal**: Becoming a source of emotional or financial support for one or both parents.

- **Financial concerns**: Worrying about their parents' ability to manage finances independently or the impact on future inheritance.

- **Grief and loss**: Mourning the loss of family history and its effect on their own identity.

- **Relationship concerns**: Reevaluating their beliefs about marriage and questioning its permanence after watching their parents' separation.[18]

My own experience with my husband's MLC has deeply affected our children, whether anyone wants to admit it or not. How could it not? Although I didn't see the crisis coming, my kids certainly didn't either. They were blindsided as well. Instead of their parents celebrating their new careers, marriage, and independence, we were consumed by the crisis. In the beginning, I was devastated and depressed, which was something my kids didn't know how to navigate. Meanwhile, their dad appeared to be enjoying his new life. Suddenly, they were caught in the middle, forced to choose between pleasing their dad or supporting me. Although I tried to avoid putting them in that position, it was inevitable.

My oldest initially told me, "I don't want to do anything with them," referring to his dad and the affair partner. But over time, he realized that if he wanted to spend time with his dad, that meant also seeing her. He eventually said, "I'm so sorry, Mom, but I want to have a relationship with Dad." Hearing that broke my heart. He was at a crossroads, and the situation put him in an impossible position. It was agonizing to watch, but I knew I had to set my ego aside and do what was best for him. I learned to say, "I hope you have a good time," even when it hurt.

Looking back, I hope my kids see how hard I fought for our marriage of twenty-five years and that I didn't give up without trying. I tried to handle everything with grace and compassion, never putting their dad down, and attempting to understand his struggles with empathy. Of course, I wasn't perfect. There were moments I could have handled better, and my children saw those moments too. But mostly, I kept the ugliness to myself and tried to shield them from it.

Rising Stronger: Tools to Help Grow Through the Crisis

There are two key parts to navigating an MLC: 1) managing the crisis itself, figuring out how to interact with your husband and how to handle the drama, and 2) focusing on your own growth.

When your husband is in MLC and isn't at home, this is a perfect time to embark on your own journey of self-improvement. You might wonder why you should be the one to change since he is the one behaving badly and is in crisis. No one is perfect, and there is always room for growth. This isn't about changing for his benefit; it's about discovering new horizons within yourself. Each step you take toward self-awareness and healing brings you closer to becoming the best version of you.

As you stand for your marriage, remember that standing is not about waiting. You are standing with strength, not desperation. It's not about putting your life on pause or hoping your husband snaps out of it. It's about choosing to live with intention and integrity, even when everything feels uncertain. Standing is about making a conscious choice to align with your values and move forward in your own life, even when your husband is lost in his crisis. One reason women struggle with standing is because they haven't figured out their why. So, let's talk about the whys behind why some women stand:

- They know their husband isn't himself.
- To model commitment and resilience for their children.
- They believe down deep that their marriage isn't meant to end this way.

Whatever your reason, it has to come from you; not from fear, not from pressure, not from what your friends or family think you should do. Standing isn't about living in denial, it's about holding space for the possibility of healing while creating a life that is meaningful, whole, and fulfilling... no matter what happens. In my Resilient Hearts Membership Group (https://www.standingspouses.com/resilient-hearts), we spend real time figuring out your personal whys. During one of our group calls, which my friends, Jennifer and Grace, co-lead with me, Jennifer introduced a self-inventory exercise that turned out to be so powerful and eye-opening that I knew I had to share it here too.

Start with Self-Reflection

Take a look at who you are and who you want to become. This isn't about blaming yourself for your husband's MLC. It's about taking responsibility for your own growth. Create an Admiration Inventory of five people you admire, friends, family, coworkers, or mentors, and write down one trait you admire in each of them. Why do those traits resonate with you? Use that list to help shape future you.

What changes do you need to make to get closer to that version of yourself? Do the internal work to become the ideal you that you want to be. Take an honest inventory of your own behavior. Do you complain a lot? Placing a marble in a jar for each complaint works wonders for tracking this. Do you listen, or just wait for your turn to talk? This could indicate a need to be seen and validated. Do you gossip or speak negatively about others? Perhaps this reveals unmet emotional needs, like a desire to bond or feel superior to help soothe insecurity. Do you prioritize your own self-care, or do you run on fumes and martyrdom? This often means you've tied your worth to being needed, productive, or indispensable at the cost of your emotional, physical, and spiritual well-being.

Standing gives you the opportunity to become the best version of you, not for your husband, but for yourself. Make this one of your mantras: "I stand because it aligns with who I am, not because of what he's doing."

Let Go of Resentment and Reclaim Your Power

Letting go of blame and resentment is one of the hardest parts of this journey, especially if anger is your go-to-emotion. It's ok to feel that fire of emotion, but you don't want to live in it every day. That hurts you more than it hurts anyone else.

Start by asking:

- Am I replaying old hurts that I could have handled differently?
- Am I holding onto patterns where I gave up my boundaries?
- Am I blaming him for things I actually said "yes" to when I should have said "no"?

Jennifer told us she used The Forgive Process (a process created by Lee Baucom in his program "Save the Marriage") to release years of resentment, and it completely shifted how she saw her situation. Once she worked through the past, the fresh pain from her husband's crisis became easier to process, not because it didn't hurt, but because she had changed the way she carried it.

Jennifer, Grace, and I created and hosted a workshop called, "How to Stay Sane During Your Husband's Midlife Crisis." Out of those conversations, we created a set of guiding principles we call, The 10 Golden Rules of Standing (Jennifer's idea). These are simple, practical, and powerful reminders you can lean on when the rollercoaster of MLC feels like it is too much to handle. These rules will keep you grounded, resilient, and focused on who you want to become, no matter how chaotic the climb may feel.

The 10 Golden Rules of Standing

1. Self-care is critical to your survival. Don't skimp on it. Put your oxygen mask on first before putting your kids' mask on. Happiness is an inside job.

2. Live in the present. Don't dwell on the past or obsess about what might happen in the future.

3. Don't make decisions in emotional spirals. If you are waffling (trying to decide whether you want to give up or

not), give yourself forty-eight hours before making any major decisions.

4. Stop seeking outside validation. Your clarity won't come from social media, well-meaning friends, or family. It comes from within.

5. Shift your mind and change your questions. Instead of asking, "What if he never comes back?" try asking, "Who do I want to be in this moment?"

6. Write out your whys: your reasons for standing. Create your own personal standing mantra. Something like: "I stand because it aligns with my values. I am not waiting; I'm growing while holding space for my marriage."

7. Don't take things personally. This MLC is not about you.

8. Look for humor. There's plenty in the craziness of MLC. Find it.

9. Be unpredictable. Try new things, get out of your routines.

10. Take pride in your appearance. Just a little extra care improves your confidence and self-esteem.

The Golden Rules aren't about being perfect, they're about helping you stay grounded, connected to yourself, and strong through the ups and downs of this journey. As my friend Grace says, "Standing is a process. It's something that gets stronger over time. You don't have to make a life and death decision about standing in the beginning. First, process your pain, so you can cultivate empathy. You have to build yourself up to stand." Standing is not the same as being passive. It's rooted in values and guided by strength. Standing is active, not reactive. It's not about tolerating bad behavior, excusing emotional abuse, or letting your husband walk all over you. You have to set boundaries for yourself, not for him. If he's monstering or being unkind, you can set a boundary and calmly say, "I'm going to take a walk. Maybe we can talk when things have settled a bit." That's not being a doormat, that's protecting your peace.

Pay attention to your thoughts. Waffling starts in your mind, when you're constantly exposed to negativity through music, movies, social media, or even well-meaning friends and family. Be intentional about what you let into your mental space. You are not going to be 100 percent every day. Some days, it might feel like you're barely at 1 percent, and that's exactly when you need to go back and reread the whys you wrote down. They are there for a reason; to help you thrive... today, not someday.

If you are waiting to start living until your husband comes back, you will be miserable, not to mention stuck. Go skiing. Go to the farmers' market. Try the new sushi place. Create a life you love now, not later. Resentment grows when you let your life shrink. You don't need permission to enjoy your life. You're allowed to thrive, even during the storm. Your life is happening now. Don't miss it waiting for someday. Your growth is not about earning his love back, it's about becoming the woman you want to be; someone who listens, lifts others up, sets boundaries, and takes care of herself. When you become that woman, your life feels fuller and freer, whether he finds his way back or not.

You Are Not the Cause, But You Can Contribute to the Solution

Your husband's MLC is not your fault. But every marriage has patterns, some healthy, some not. It takes humility and honesty to examine your own role in those patterns. Books like *The Empowered Wife*, *The Surrendered Wife*, *Male Midlife Crisis*, and *Men Made Easy* helped me understand the fundamental differences in how men and women operate. Learning to appreciate those differences changed everything for me, not only in my marriage, but in all my relationships, as did my practicum and work with Brooke Castillo.

Many of the following simple but powerful practices were inspired by those books, Hearts Blessing's website, and by the mindset work I did through Brooke Castillo's teachings. They became anchors for me during the hardest parts of the journey. These simple practices can help you stay grounded and true to yourself. Remember, standing strong doesn't mean doing everything perfectly, it means showing up with intention.

- **Express gratitude** for what he does, even if it's tiny at the moment. Catch the good and say thanks.

- **Avoid public criticism.** Nothing cuts deeper than feeling embarrassed. When your criticism is directed at your husband publicly (whether he is present or not), that's called emasculation. Laura Doyle speaks a lot about this in her books. Instead, build him up, especially in front of your children, friends, and family.

- **Let go of control**, even when it's uncomfortable. Have no expectations. Release the urge to manage his behavior, predict his next move, or control the outcome. When you let go of all of this, you can focus on your peace, not his actions.

- **Respect his role as a provider**, even if you're one too. Honor the contribution he makes to your household and the entire family. As mentioned earlier, society puts a lot of pressure on men in this area. This issue shows up in almost all of my clients' stories.

- **Prioritize your own joy and well-being.** Your happiness isn't selfish, it's essential.

- **Standing is a long game.** So even if you are doing all the things, you will not see the outcome right away. No matter what happens, you will be better for standing as long as you focus on yourself.

Growth is the goal, no matter what happens. At the end of the day, standing is about *you*. Your peace. Your healing. Your wholeness. It's about doing the work so that no matter what your husband chooses, you walk away stronger, wiser, and more grounded in who you are.

So, what's your why for standing?

If you knew without a doubt that your husband would return one day, would you be proud of how you handled this season? Would you be proud of how you showed up for yourself? That's your guidepost. And that's your power.

What to Do Now

If you are choosing to stand, write down your whys for standing. Be honest and specific. Why are you choosing to stand? What values are guiding that decision? This isn't about what your friends or family think, it's about what you know deep in your heart.

"I choose to stand because _____"

Identify your survival brain versus your evolved brain moments. Begin to notice when you're operating from fear and survival (crying on the bathroom floor, scrolling Facebook for clues, panicking over timelines). Then tune in to the whispers from your evolved brain, the part of you that is dreaming bigger.

"Today, my survival brain said _____."

My evolved brain reminded me that _____."

Take a tiny step toward self-care. You don't need a 10-step plan. Just pick one thing. Shower. Take a walk. Stretch. This isn't about productivity, it's about showing up for you.

"What is one thing can I do today that honors me?" _____

Do the Admiration Inventory. Choose five people you admire. Write out the traits they have that speak to you. These are clues to who you want to become.

What qualities do I want to grow into during this season?

1. _____

2. _____

3. _____

4. _____

5. _____

Work on letting go of resentment (gently). Start asking yourself where you might need to forgive, release, or simply stop replaying old stories.

"What thought or memory is hurting me more than helping me?"

_____

"What's one way I can release it?" _____

You don't need to do all of this today. Start where you are, with what you have. Even 1 percent effort is enough when your heart is healing. You've got this, and I've got you.

Key Takeaways

- It's not about you, but it's all up to you. Your husband's MLC isn't your fault, but your healing, growth, and happiness are still your responsibility. You can't control his chaos, but you can reclaim your power and rewrite your story.

- Standing for your marriage is an active choice, not a passive one. It doesn't mean sitting around waiting in misery. It means choosing growth, honoring your values, and building a beautiful life now, even while holding space for your husband.

- Your survival brain clings to the familiar, even if it's painful. Listen to your evolved brain by tapping into your prefrontal cortex, which helps you envision a brighter, more fulfilling future.

- You must know your why for standing. Standing from a place of desperation leads to pain and burnout. When you root your why in values, faith, and inner strength standing for your marriage becomes an empowering decision, even on the hard days.

- Midlife crisis impacts the whole family. Divorce or even the chaos of separation affects kids deeply, even adult kids.

- Healing isn't just about the marriage, it's about you. Working on yourself isn't about winning your husband back, it's about becoming a woman you deeply admire. That transformation becomes the real reward of the journey, no matter the outcome.

Chapter 5.

NAVIGATING THE TREACHEROUS TRAIL: DEALING WITH THE AFFAIR PARTNER

She may have his attention right now, but she will never have your history, your heart, or your healing.

~ Anonymous

efore we go any further, I want to prepare your heart for what's ahead. If you're standing for your marriage, an affair partner is one of the toughest obstacles you'll encounter on this journey. In the beginning, it may seem like she holds all of the power: the power to break your heart, steal your husband, and destroy the life you built. But I need you to hear this loud and clear: she is not the cause of your husband's MLC. She is only one piece, a symptom of a much larger puzzle. It's natural to think, "If only she were gone, everything would be ok." But even if she disappears tomorrow, your husband's internal struggle will still be raging. His confusion, his restlessness, his anger, didn't start with her and they won't end with her either.

Finding out about an affair feels like losing a limb; it's excruciating, gut-wrenching, and leaves you questioning how you'll ever function again. Everything you know feels ripped away, and life, as you imagined it, seems shattered. But as you move through the journey, your perspective starts to shift. You begin to realize that while losing a limb is devastating, the bigger goal is keeping the body alive: your marriage, your family, and your sanity. Saving the body becomes the priority because, as hard as it is to live without a limb, losing the entire body would be far worse. With time, you start to see that even though the wound runs deep, healing is possible and you're stronger than you thought you were. Likely, before that happens, you will go through a difficult time when you might question your decision to stand for your marriage. Personally, I had to survive the raw devastation of a double betrayal before healing ever felt possible.

The Treacherous Trail of Betrayal

No doubt about it, finding out about my husband's affair, and the years that followed, were absolutely worst years of my life. I call them "the muck years" because everyone just wanted to know the dirt and gossip about its current events: where they were going, what they were doing together, how she taunted me. The more you get wrapped up in that, the more negative your life becomes. It becomes a frenzy with everyone. My heart was ripped out of my chest and stomped on repeatedly. Not only did I have to deal with my husband's infidelity, but I also had to deal with being stabbed in the back by a friend of ten years, the affair partner. In so many ways, that hurt much worse because I knew my husband was crazy, going through a crisis, and had lost his mind. But my friend? There was no excuse. Even if he had moved out. You don't date your friend's husband of twenty-three years. As my daughter-in-law said, "She broke the Girl Code!"

My former friend and I spent many evenings together. Mostly, she came over for dinner, and we talked, just the two of us. She didn't cook and I did, so I would always make her a nice meal. We would have dinner and wine and talk. My husband was never around on our girl nights. He was usually upstairs working or playing games. Over those ten years, there were only a handful of times when the four of us, my husband and me, plus her and her boyfriend, went out to dinner or boating together. Later, I was told information that made me realize this wasn't the first time she had crossed boundaries in relationships. Whether or not every detail was true, it shattered my trust. What mattered was how profoundly it shook me to realize the friendship I thought was safe wasn't what I believed it to be.

My husband actually told me he wanted space and moved out before the affair. He technically didn't date her until a few months later, but I knew they had been spending time together before then. The year my husband moved out, and the next year that followed, were the hardest part of the entire MLC experience for me. It tore me apart to realize that the man I had done everything with for the past twenty-five years suddenly didn't want to do anything with me. It was as if, overnight, his feelings for me had changed. It hurt, and the pain was excruciating. It was pure grief. Looking back, the muck years are a part of my story that helped me grow. They were the beginning of my transformation. It was horrible, but I survived and now I'm happy to say I am finally thriving. Somehow, slowly, the broken pieces came together and healed into a much stronger heart, but not until I came to terms with the affair partner.

So much of the left behind spouse's time in the beginning is figuring out how to deal with the idea of her and not get caught up in her existence. In many of the MLC forums, many women find it helpful to give the affair partner a nickname, like *troll, mattress, or LO* (short for limerent object). Renaming her can help your brain cope differently because it depersonalizes her. In my case, since I knew her as my former best friend, this was definitely a good thing. When you give her a different name, you don't compare her to you, which is what you want to do instinctually. In the beginning, you may feel she is a replacement for you, but she's not, which is why it helps to name her. Giving her a nickname takes away the power your mind tries to give her. It separates her from you and helps stop you from falling into the trap of comparison. She's not "the other you" or some upgraded version; she's just a woman caught up in your husband's crisis. Depersonalizing her helps you control of how much mental space she gets to occupy in your mind.

She drew my husband in, using the same charm she once used on me. Back in high school, I was a classic overachiever: the straight-A student who never quite fit in with the popular crowd. She made me feel like I belonged, like I was part of something exclusive. It wasn't that she made me feel particularly special, but she had a way of making people feel cool, included, and accepted. She was that magnetic, popular type everyone wanted to be around, and I wasn't immune to her pull. That's how she eventually won over my husband. For nearly nine years, my husband barely noticed her, and I had always assumed he wasn't particularly fond of her. When they eventually started getting along, I was actually relieved. I thought it was a positive change. I trusted her completely and often confided in her, sharing how lucky I felt to have such a great husband. We'd talk about her terrible dates (she used many of the dating apps), and I would tell her, "I couldn't even imagine dating now. My husband is the love of my life." Sadly, I trusted her and even opened up once about my confusion when I couldn't make sense of my husband's behavior, never suspecting she was already setting her sights on him.

A few weeks after he moved out, she and I went to dinner. I thought she was there to listen and be my friend. When I told her I was not giving up on my marriage of twenty-two years (at the time), she told me, "You need to move on." That's when I knew. I really knew. She had moved in on my husband. Good friends don't tell you to move on when your husband has just moved out. Good friends listen; they tell you it's going to be ok. Good friends help you stand for your marriage if that's what you choose. They don't say, "You need to move on" only a few weeks after you are separated. After that conversation, I started putting the pieces together, recalling times when she needed his help to move a few things in his truck, building her trellis, or when he took her home after our girls nights and it took longer than expected. That's when I knew she was pursuing him.

Men who have gone through MLC express that they don't feel like they can talk to their wives or their friends about this dark period in their life. It's easier to talk to strangers you meet at a bar or other women you work with. Most of them don't even mean to go down the road to infidelity. In fact, it doesn't usually start out that way at all. Often, it starts out innocently by helping someone out, or a casual conversation at the office, or seeing an old high school girlfriend by chance. She appeals to his sense of masculinity. She has a small problem and the husband thinks, "Ooh I can help you; I can fix that." Now you see how she gets in. I'm pretty sure that's what happened in my husband's case. Building her a trellis during COVID lockdown. A little smile, a little flirting, and instant attachment called "limerence."

Limerence is that intoxicating feeling you get when you first fall in love, that obsessive, can't get enough, can't be apart stage when everything about the other person seems perfect and you don't recognize any flaws. When your husband is deep in MLC, he may experience this with an affair partner. Eventually, as he starts to come out of the fog, reality sets in. The fantasy crumbles, the masks fall off, and she starts making demands. Over time—sometimes years—he begins to see she isn't the devoted, understanding partner he thought she was. Instead, he realizes she is driven by her own needs, whether it's validation, control, excitement, wealth, or simply the thrill that he wants her over you. This is why MLC lasts so long, because the MLCer is convinced that their affair partner is the one who truly gets him and is there to support his new life and reinvention of himself. In reality, she is just fulfilling her own agenda. Even if they've broken up, it can take a long time for him to fully grasp that she was never the answer he thought she was.

In truth, the affair partner serves as a temporary rescuer to take your husband's mind off his MLC. One of my clients recently sent me a Facebook video from Dr. Kathy Nickerson. In it, she talked about affairs and how affairs are "painkillers to treat their (husband's) emotional pain by getting this attention, this fantasy, this validation. They feel better so they don't notice this emotional pain as much."[19] The affair partner is a good distraction because she listens and dotes solely on him. In the beginning she is not demanding, she's easy and free. That's what makes her so attractive to him. Later, she might ask for money, expect gifts, and hint at trips they could take together to escape the stress he is under. He has no responsibility to her, which is a big deal for him. Remember, he feels burdened by all the responsibilities he already has—home, family, wife, work—and he is seeking an escape. With her, he feels free. Typically, that's all it is, an immature relationship, someone to do something with, a new person who listens without questioning him. This can also happen online.

Not every spouse in MLC has a physical affair. Sometimes, it can be an emotional one. However, some men in MLC don't ever have affairs. But most do. They can fall in "luv" (as Hearts Blessing puts it, meaning temporary limerence) with someone they have never even met because the person listens. As one left behind spouse said, "The lure of the affair partner is essentially a quick fix" to their MLC brain.

The Affair Partner vs. The Real Issue: Your Husband's Crisis

While it's tempting to focus on an affair partner and to see her as the villain in the story, the cold, hard truth is that your husband's MLC is the real issue. She is only a distraction that makes him feel better for the time being. Many spouses believe the misconception that the affair is about sex when, in fact, it isn't. The affair is about your husband's lack of connection with you and his own inner emptiness he is trying to fill.

You might think, "Well, I listen. We talk. We have date night." But somewhere along the way, the two of you have lost that intimate (not necessarily sexual) connection you once had. You have lost your true and sincere gratitude for one another. This works both ways. Perhaps early in your marriage, you praised his every action, and that fed his ego. Over the years, you have stopped doing that, most likely because you assume he knows how you feel about him. He might perceive this as a lack of gratitude. You get out of the habit of being grateful, of noticing all the nice things he does, even those small, common, everyday things. You might think, "I don't need to thank him for doing the dishes; I do the dishes all the time and he never thanks me. So, why should I thank him?" Although that might be a fair argument, it ignores the reality that presents itself for many spouses of MLCers. They miss that attention, gratitude, and praise.

Interestingly, it goes both ways. He has lost it for you as well. Try to recall the last time your husband complimented you on your appearance, congratulated you for an accomplishment, or thanked you for doing something simple. He wants to be your rock, your favorite guy, the one you confide in, even the one you need, but he can't verbalize what's going on. Over the years, you have probably outgrown needing him for this validation, but he hasn't outgrown the need to give it to you. He just doesn't know how or whether you still need or appreciate it. According to Kara Oh, "He doesn't know what to do because he doesn't understand that his feelings of dissatisfaction aren't about you; they're about his inability to feel. So, too often, he assumes that he doesn't love [you] any longer and starts to pursue his need for love elsewhere. But more partners, more sex, and more climaxes will not give him what he seeks."[20]

Unfortunately, he doesn't realize that seeking the attention he craves from an outside source won't satisfy what's really missing inside of him. So, for a time, the affair partner satisfies his need for validation without him having to reciprocate because he has no responsibility to her. Most people assume an affair is all about sex, but in reality, it's about intimacy and connection, or at least the illusion of it. Midlife crisis husbands aren't just looking for physical excitement; they are searching for someone who makes them feel seen, understood, and validated. Affair partners often provide this deep emotional connection, not because they are special, but because they don't carry the weight of real life in the way the wife does. There are no bills to pay, no kids to raise, no past resentments. The affair is a fantasy bubble where the MLC husband feels admired, important, and free from responsibility.

So how does this connect to intimacy skills? In her book *The Empowered Wife*, Laura Doyle teaches the six intimacy skills, designed to foster deeper connection in marriage:

1. Relinquishing Control. Instead of trying to control or change your husband, focus on your own happiness and letting go of micromanaging.

2. Respect. Show respect in your words, tone, and actions when you don't agree with him.

3. Self-Care. Prioritize your happiness, passions, and well-being.

4. Receiving Graciously. Accept love, compliments, and help without criticism or dismissal.

5. Vulnerability. Express your feelings and desires openly and authentically without blame or demand. "I would love XYZ" instead of making complaints.

6. Gratitude and Focus on the Positive. Appreciate and acknowledge what he does right instead of focusing on what he does wrong.

I've adapted the intimacy skills above for women navigating their husband's MLC from Laura Doyle's book, *The Empowered Wife*.

Laura Doyle's approach is controversial in some circles because it emphasizes a traditionally feminine approach to marriage. However, men and women do process and hear things differently. Although you may not fully agree with her methods, they are very effective in fostering better communication because many husbands are more receptive to this style of interaction. I highly suggest reading her book in order to improve your communication skills during this MLC time.

Most wives may be missing the benefit of approaching interaction with their husband in this way without even knowing it. For example, here are some common phrases and behaviors that undermine, manipulate, smother, and criticize rather than show your husband respect. Have you ever said any of these phrases?

- "Here, just let me do it!" Even if you're trying to be helpful, this makes him feel incapable.
- "Why are we going this way? It's faster to go ..." This shows a lack of trust. (I did this one a lot!)
- "Are you sure you want to do it this way?"
- "I knew that wouldn't work."
- "That's not how it happened." Correcting his storytelling in public.
- "Why don't you text me more?"
- "Oh, I already RSVP'd for both of us."
- Making him lunch, buying him clothes, etc. This suggests you don't trust him to make his own decisions.

All of these phrases can make your husband feel incapable, show a lack of trust, or both.

These little things add up over time. What may seem like harmless comments or actions can slowly chip away at connection and respect in a marriage. You likely didn't mean any harm. You were just trying to help, communicate, or keep things running smoothly. But over the years, these patterns can make a husband feel incompetent, untrusted, or controlled, even if that was never your intention. And this is where *she* comes in.

The affair partner doesn't carry the history, the responsibilities, or the emotional baggage of real life. She offers validation, admiration and excitement, all the things he may have convinced himself were missing at home. But that doesn't mean she's better than you are. It means she's new, untested, and telling him exactly what he wants to hear. Realizing this isn't about blaming yourself, it's about recognizing how emotional distance builds over time. Just as these little things may have contributed to his disconnection, small positive shifts can also start to rebuild it. This is where her intimacy skills come in.

As difficult as it might seem, try practicing a few of these skills when your MLC husband makes an effort to connect with you. You're not meeting him halfway; you're not negotiating a relationship right now. What you are doing is working on your side of the emotional bridge, shifting how you show up. When you start interacting differently—when you are calm instead of reactive, gracious instead of resentful, grounded instead of desperate—he begins to experience you differently. This subtle shift can start to change the story he tells himself about you, your marriage, and even about his own actions. Remember, your work is not about chasing him or understanding the affair, it's about restoring the emotional connection through your own growth. You're not doing this to win him back. You're doing it because you have chosen to rise higher, no matter what he's doing. This new approach is not about performing or pretending, it's about being your best self: calm, grounded, and wise. Little by little, connection builds when you show up from that place, no matter where he is on his journey.

As you make the choice to operate from a higher place, please resist the urge to seek out the affair partner. Some left behind wives have gone to extreme lengths to uncover the affair partner's identity, sometimes with success, other times not so much. The energy involved in this kind of pursuit can be emotionally draining, not to mention financially costly. Just don't do it. Many wives are under the assumption that the affair partner is fully aware that the person they are intimately involved with is married when, in fact, some affair partners don't even know. He might remove his wedding ring or tell others he is separated in an effort to present himself as a single person. Although this seems like the ultimate act of betrayal, remember that he is trying to figure himself out, maybe to reinvent himself. Therefore, any reminders of his current or previous life threaten the new version of himself he is trying to create.

On the other hand, many affair partners—like my former best friend—do know the relationship status of the person they are attracted to, and they pursue them anyway. Whatever the case, you don't need to know who she is. In fact, it's best you don't. Just know, she is nothing like you. Most times, she is quite the opposite of you. This is an indication of your husband testing the waters, trying to find out what else is out there, what else can fill the internal void he has been living with. He is just grasping at straws, and she is an obvious, available straw that has presented itself at the time.

One final note of warning: Do not give into the temptation to contact her. You'll only drive your spouse closer to her. You may feel an overwhelming urge to confront her, expose her, or demand answers. You might believe that if you could just make her see the damage she's causing, she would back off, or that if you shame her enough, she'll feel guilty and leave him alone. That's not how it works. If you reach out to her, you hand her the power. She will use it to play the victim and to tell your husband that you are being controlling and unreasonable. In most cases, affair partners thrive on the drama. Your reaction only fuels their role as the only one who understands him. If she enjoys the chase, she'll use your anger as proof that he should pull further away from you. It becomes the "us versus you" story. Even if she isn't manipulative, your words won't change her mind at all. She has already justified the affair in her head. No matter what you say, she is convinced she's the exception.

More importantly, your husband—not her—is the one who made vows to you. If anyone should be held accountable, it's him. The best way to shift the dynamic is to focus on your own strength and dignity, not on her. You don't need her to lose in order for you to win. You are already winning every time you choose dignity over drama.

Children and the Affair Partner

This is one of the really sucky parts of living through your husband's MLC. I don't think it matters if your children are young, or older like mine, the experience is extremely hard on them in different but equally painful ways.

For younger children, their world is built on security, routine, and the belief that their parents are a team. When their dad starts acting differently, becoming distant, angry, or even moving out, it shatters their sense of stability. They don't have the emotional maturity to process why Daddy is pulling away from them, so they often internalize and blame themselves, thinking they did something wrong. Even if you reassure them that Daddy's behavior is not their fault, they still feel the tension and confusion.

For older children, especially teenagers and adults, the pain may be different but just as intense. While they may have a better understanding of what is happening, that fact doesn't make it any easier for them to process or handle the situation. Actually, in some ways it can be harder as they can feel like the MLC is a betrayal to them as well as to their mom. Their dad isn't the man they thought he was. Their "superhero" has fallen. Watching him prioritize his own crisis or choosing activities with the affair partner over the family, can create anger, resentment, and deep emotional wounds. Adult children also struggle with divided loyalties, feeling the pressure to stay neutral while secretly feeling hurt and abandoned.

If an affair is part of your husband's MLC, it's best not to talk about the affair partner with your children, if possible. At least don't tell them everything you know. To help keep things neutral, you could simply say: "Dad is just going through a hard time right now. We love him despite everything he's done." Kids will follow your lead. Try to be respectful when speaking about your husband to your kids. Don't put him down in front of them. You don't have to mention an affair; however, sometimes acknowledging that there is another woman in their dad's life is inevitable. Allow them to draw their own conclusions about that situation or encourage them to ask their dad to explain what is happening. After all, having the affair is a choice your husband has made for himself; he should be able to explain his actions to some degree to his children. It is not your responsibility to help your children understand infidelity, the affair partner, or what this means for the future of your family.

Although I didn't want to, I ended up telling our kids about the affair partner. They already knew her as my best friend, so she wasn't a stranger to them. They went to the same gym as her son, and I didn't want them to find out from someone else. Not only was it hard on my kids, but her son was also very upset. Her son even contacted me because he thought I didn't know about the affair. My heart was ripped apart by his texts to me, not for my sake, but for his. He was devastated. He looked up to my husband as a mentor, so in a way, he was impacted in the same way my kids were. My oldest basically hid his head in the sand and pretended not to know anything. If I ever said anything about what was going on, he would say, "Mom, just go find a new husband."

My youngest defended his dad for a long time. "That's his life and his decisions." I respected the way he handled it, but when I moved out of state, he chose to come with me, mostly because he was worried about me being on my own. Later, after my son broke up with his first real girlfriend, he began to understand how much the affair impacted me because he and his girlfriend would talk every day and then, suddenly, they didn't. It drove home for him how devastating it was to have someone you love suddenly disappear and seem to want nothing to do with you. Of course, I tried not to let him see me upset, but that was nearly impossible since we lived under the same roof. I did my best not to put both of them in the middle, but I know it still happened at times.

Some kids refuse to talk to their dad once they find out about the affair partner. They also turn down invitations to go to dinner with their dad and the affair partner, refuse to invite them to graduations and other events, and decline to do anything with their dad if the affair partner is involved. If that is how they feel, and they are older, support their decision. Let them be in charge of their relationship with their dad. I am grateful that my kids continued to have a relationship with their dad despite all of the unusual behavior during his MLC. My husband worked hard to make sure he spent time with our kids, which meant a lot to me, and I'm sure to the kids as well.

No matter their age, kids experience MLC differently than we do. While you're mourning the loss of the marriage you once had, they are mourning the loss of the father and family unit they once knew. Holidays and celebrations are not the same. Unlike you, they may not have the ability to detach, set boundaries, or find a support group. They just feel the fallout.

Stay Out of the Drama

While the affair partner may not be the cause of your husband's MLC, she often adds fuel to the fire, creating drama in both his life and yours, if you allow her to. She can act as a wedge, discouraging your husband from staying connected to his family by trying to prioritize her needs above your family's, making it difficult for him to participate in holidays, birthdays, or other special events.

Many affair partners will say or do whatever it takes to pull the husband further away, often encouraging divorce with promises like, "It will bring closure; you'll feel better." Some even resort to manipulation by withholding sex and affection or using it as leverage to get what they want. In extreme cases, they may go as far as getting pregnant or threatening self-harm to maintain control. I wouldn't have believed these stories if I hadn't heard them shared over and over again in MLC support groups. The manipulation is real, but it's important to remember that her behavior is not your battle to fight. The best thing you can do is focus on your own boundaries and healing.

How do you deal with the affair partner? You don't.

One left behind spouse sent me this: "These affair partners try to claim what is not theirs. They even attempt to buy your kids stuff despite them telling her they want nothing to do with her. Despite all that, the husbands text and check in with you. They send flowers and try to ensure you are provided for," she explained. Of her own experience, she added, "Mine sent me money, bought gifts, and would call me for hours each day while he was on the road. He just couldn't let go. On the other hand, he didn't want to let go of his new gal either. She was fun, free. Of course, this behavior isn't fair to the left behind spouse or to the affair partner. Can you imagine being with a man who is constantly worried about his wife or ex's well-being? If you were the affair partner, why would you want someone who is married and going through a crisis and unable to commit solely to you?"

The affair partner wants to be liked and accepted, so she works on your kids as well as on your husband, buying them expensive gifts, texting them, trying to push her way into your family's life. It can be a game for some of them, and so many times once they get what they want, they drop your husband.

The truth is, however, that most often the affair partner is broken too. That's part of why your spouse and them are attracted to each other in the beginning. I have tried hard to find some empathy for my husband's affair partner because clearly, she has her own issues if she continues to choose men who are unavailable. But I'll be honest, finding that empathy isn't easy. If you wonder why I might even want to try and find empathy for her, here's the reason. Empathy isn't about excusing her behavior; it's about freeing yourself. When you see her as another hurting human instead of the monster in your story, she loses power to consume your thoughts. That said, I'll admit, I haven't found that empathy yet, especially since she was once my friend. But at the end of the day, you have to let it all go and stay out of the drama. This is not yours to fix.

So, how do you deal with the affair partner? You don't. Try to think about her as little as possible. It's so hard in the beginning. On days when I was really angry, I read Hearts Blessing's post, "I. Am. The. Wife."[21] over and over. That helped me immensely. I also would journal and get it all out on paper. Doing the thought work that I teach in my course, and learning how to manage your mind, helps a lot. Remember that she is not the problem, she's only a symptom of the crisis. Letting go of her wasn't easy for me, but it was absolutely necessary. At the time, I often felt manipulated and pushed further away from my husband. When I saw certain posts on social media, they felt like subtle digs meant to provoke me. Over time, I realized that engaging with those feelings, even mentally, only kept me stuck in pain.

One of the best things you can do during this time is to avoid "pain shopping." Don't go looking for trouble. Do not obsess over her social media or your husband's social media. Don't drive by her house or your husband's apartment. Remind yourself that she is a temporary escape for your husband, not a solution to his inner struggles. The real problem is his MLC, a storm you can't control. Once you shift your focus away from her and onto your own healing, you will find peace. It will take time, but eventually you will stop caring about what they are doing, and you will start to live your own life. The truth is, she's not worth your energy. Don't get caught up in all of that ugliness because it won't bring you peace; it will only feed the fire of hate. And hate accomplishes nothing. I finally learned that, but it took me a long time.

There are two critical things to remember when it comes to the affair partner (or whatever name you prefer):

1. Avoid contacting her. Do not engage in any form of communication: no calls, texts, emails, or social media messages. Even if she reaches out to you, do not respond. No good will come from it. She will either twist your words, play the victim, or use it as an opportunity to drive a wedge between you and your husband. Even if you feel justified in telling her exactly what you think of her, your actions will only make it look like you are the "crazy wife" while she gets to play the role of being the understanding and reasonable one. In our membership, we say, "Don't give her any oxygen." Let her expose herself on her own.

2. Resist discussing her with your husband. I know it's tempting. You want to know why he chose her, what he sees in her, or whether he's starting to see the cracks in the fantasy. Maybe you want to remind him of her faults, expose her lies, or make him see that she's manipulating him. But don't. I tried a few times and was shut down. Here's the cold, hard truth: Every time you bring her up, you reinforce her importance in his mind. So don't do it.

The best thing you can do is to shift the focus on yourself and your family because holding onto hate and bitterness only keeps you stuck. If she's truly his "soulmate," (spoiler alert: she's not), he doesn't need you to point out her flaws. The mask will fall down eventually, and he will see them for himself. But if he senses that you're constantly fixated on her, he'll defend her. The best thing you can do is to be indifferent. Nothing kills an affair fantasy faster than when it stops feeling dramatic, forbidden, and "us against the world." So, as hard as it is, don't engage. She will reveal who she really is at some point. You don't have to do a thing.

Many of my clients are terrified that their husband will marry the affair partner. However, these affairs rarely lead to the fairytale ending the affair partner might imagine. The initial excitement burns out, reality sets in, and eventually, the cracks in the relationship start to show.

"While conclusive research and studies are still sparse on this matter, the probability of an affair ending in marriage is very, very low. Based on the data available, it is between 3-5 percent. Of those affairs that do end in marriage, most join the 75 percent of second marriages that fail, which is significantly higher than first marriages."[22] Even more telling, "A second marriage that begins with infidelity is very likely heading to divorce within two years."[23]

This is one of the hardest mountains you will ever have to climb, and believe me, I've been there. The path is steep, the air is thin, and there will be moments when you wonder if you have anything left to give. But keep going. Once you reach the top, it's a game-changer. Suddenly, you can see the entire MLC for what it really is, not just the pain, but the patterns, the fears, and the illusions. That's when the view of your life expands, and you realize just how much strength you've gained along the way. You're not the same woman who started this journey. You're wiser. You're stronger. While the road behind you was so brutal, the road ahead is filled with confidence you never knew you had. Because once you've conquered this mountain, once you realize she's just an external solution and that she has nothing over you, you'll know, without a doubt, that you can handle whatever comes next.

What to Do Now

- Do not talk to the affair partner, nor text her, call her, or hunt her down.
- Do not talk about her with your husband.
- If kids are involved, don't put them in the middle. Avoid badmouthing your husband or the affair partner in front of your kids.
- You be you, shiny, happy you.
- Show him that you have a life without him. Post pictures of your life with your kids, friends, your family, and his family.

Key Takeaways

- Accept the fact that the affair partner exists. She's not the cause, she's a distraction.
- The affair partner is not about sex, it's about lost connection. She's a temporary painkiller to numb the emotions he does not want to face.
- How do you deal with her? You don't.

You've mapped out your next steps. Now it's time to find the people who will help you climb.

Chapter 6.

SCALING THE MOUNTAIN: FINDING SUPPORT AND FACING CRITICS ON YOUR JOURNEY

You don't need everyone to understand your climb. You just need someone to believe you can make it.

~ Anonymous

S tanding for your marriage during your husband's MLC is like climbing a mountain in the dark: no map, no guide, and a backpack full of judgment, doubt, and grief. If you don't have the right support system in place, you could easily lose your footing. But here's the truth: You don't need a crowd behind you. You just need a core group, a solid, grounded, soul-nourishing circle that can walk with you, even if it's just one person and a whole lot of faith.

The Quiet Power of Support

Support doesn't always roar. Sometimes it whispers, "I believe you." "You're not crazy." "This won't break you."

In the beginning, you may not know where to find this support. And honestly, some of the people you thought would be there won't be. That's not your fault. It's just what happens when life gets too real for others. But some people will rise. Unexpected allies. Online friends. Family members who surprise you. Coaches and mentors who say the exact right thing you didn't know you needed to hear. Then there's you. Don't forget you. You may not feel it right now, but you'll be one of your most loyal, unshakable sources of strength.

The Strength of Those Who Came Before

During the early MLC years, my aunt gave me my grandmother's ring. It was kind of gaudy for the current times—big with six birthstone gems—one to represent my mom, uncle, and all the grandkids. I remember when my grandmother received it. She was so happy to have her kids and grandkids all represented in one ring. After she passed, I had no idea where it went until my aunt gave it to me. I was so grateful to have it during this time in my life, not because of how it looked, but because of what it represented: strength, resilience, and legacy.

Both of my grandmothers were of hearty stock; tough cookies, as they say. But Granny was something else. Her first husband died when my mom was two and my uncle was eight. She had to leave my mom with the neighbor while she went to work at a glove factory. Later, when my mom was in sixth grade, Granny remarried. Tragically, her second husband died of a heart attack only eight months later. She lived alone the rest of her life, eventually retiring from the glove factory. She never complained. She just kept going. She lived alone for more than forty-five years and passed at age ninety-two. So, when times were really hard for me, when my husband was deep in crisis and I was struggling to find my footing—I thought of her. I imagined what she might have said: "Keep going, Amy. You will make it through this. Buck up, Bucko." Granny became my secret strength, my anchor, a steady presence I could lean on when nothing else felt secure.

Building Your Support Team

You cannot survive this alone and maintain your sanity. As much as you may want to isolate yourself, to shut the world out, the truth is, you need people. Not just any people; the right people. If it weren't for my support system, I wouldn't be here. My family, in-laws, sister-in-law, soul sister friends, and mentors each held a piece of my heart, so it didn't completely shatter. That includes the support of women who came before me, even the ones who aren't here anymore. Their strength is woven into mine. So, let's talk about what kinds of support you'll need, how to navigate the people who don't understand, and what to do when you're the only one who still believes he might come back.

Family

Family can be your strongest allies, or your biggest hurdles. In the beginning, most family members don't recognize your husband's MLC for what it truly is. How could they? You barely understand it yourself. They only see the surface-level symptoms: the move out, the affair, the chaos. What they can't see is the deep internal turmoil he's hiding because most MLCers don't share that part, even with you.

That's why it's often best not to tell your family everything. Oversharing too soon usually causes more harm than help. I've heard so many women say, "My parents hate him, my sisters hate him. There's no way we can come back from this." This is normal in the beginning. If you want true support, start by gently educating them about MLC, your specific situation, and how you're choosing to handle it. Be honest but only share what you're comfortable with.

When they see that you're grounded, informed, and committed to standing for your marriage, they're more likely to follow your lead.

Here are a few tips to manage your family:

- Ask them not to bash your husband in front of you or your children.

- Tell them you don't want MLC or what they might see as your marital challenges to dominate every conversation.

- Share what you've learned about MLC slowly and patiently.

- There's a difference between "talking" about it and "gossiping." Help them understand the difference.

So, what can you say? You don't have to explain your decision, but you do want to express your firm commitment to your decision to stand for your marriage. In doing so, showing compassion for your husband sets a beautiful example for your kids. The more compassion you show your husband, the more your family will mirror that. Here is a simple response to any questions or comments your family might have about your decision to stand for your marriage: "You may not like that I'm standing for my marriage, but I am. I know you have your thoughts and opinions, but I would appreciate it if you wouldn't badmouth him in front of me or the kids. It's just not helpful to anyone."

Even though my parents weren't thrilled about me standing at first, they eventually came to understand what I meant when I said this wasn't about our marriage, that this was something deeper. My mom was so upset with my husband at first. She couldn't believe his actions, but the more I explained, the more she came to realize that what I was saying was true; it was a mental breakdown of sorts. She saw his odd behavior—how withdrawn and distant he had become, how he seemed like a stranger even in his own skin—and my dad witnessed it too. I'm so grateful that they trusted me and kept an open mind with him. It kept the relationship between them intact.

For the last five weeks of my mom's life, my husband sent her flowers every week. She was delighted every single time. The night before she passed away, she looked at the flowers and said, "I love him." She was my biggest supporter of all. She really understood him.

My aunt and uncle were also huge sources of comfort, especially on those long Friday nights when I felt lonely and needed reassuring conversation from loved ones. We'd talk, laugh, and connect without necessarily mentioning my husband. That simple connection carried me through some very difficult times. Sadly, my uncle passed during that time, but his support is still with me. And then there's my Aunt Janet. She survived her own husband's MLC and went on to have a long marriage. She passed before my husband's MLC, and though I never got to talk to her about it, I know from family that she quietly fought for her marriage and won. They were married more than fifty years. I admire her strength as she kept most of her struggle to herself.

In-laws

Not everyone has a great relationship with their in-laws. Whether you do or not, you want them on your support team. Even if things were strained before, your husband's MLC is a reason to strengthen that bond. Let me explain.

You need his family, and they need you. In the beginning, their support can help you, but later, after your husband has blown everything up, they may need yours. They will experience shame, embarrassment, and confusion, just as you did. They often feel like they have failed as parents. Reassuring them that this isn't their fault—just as it isn't yours—can help everyone cope.

Family dynamics shift radically during an MLC, often in very painful ways. Holidays change, and his siblings may be upset that things aren't the way they used to be. His parents may be upset and not want to do holidays things without him. They don't want to put up the tree this year. They don't want to host Thanksgiving. His siblings may blame him, you, or just feel resentful that their family is fractured. Your in-laws may be struggling to hold things together while also feeling lost about how to support their son.

This crisis doesn't just impact your marriage; it rips a huge hole through the entire family. There are so many left behind spouses whose in-laws blame them for their son's MLC and refuse to do anything with them. If his parents or siblings blame you or have been influenced by his words, you may need to take the lead in maintaining the connection. Invite them over, meet them for coffee, or simply send pictures or even a handwritten note. They may not yet realize how much they need you, but they do. One important thing you can do is to let them know that your relationship with them is separate from their relationship with your husband. Regardless of what happens in your marriage, they are still your family, and you want to keep that connection, for yourself and your kids and grandkids.

This crisis tears families apart. Taking small steps to keep these bonds intact can make a big difference. Even if the relationship feels strained at first, keep reaching out. Include them in holidays and family events. Your husband most likely won't attend, but that doesn't mean they shouldn't be there. His absence is hard on everyone, but maintaining family ties is worth it. Small actions matter. Invite them to dinner. Share photos of the kids. Send a kind message or card. Let them know they're still part of your life. Even if your husband is absent, they don't have to be.

I spent many holidays with my in-laws when my husband wasn't there, and it meant the world to them, to me, and to our boys. When he finally comes home, having those relationships intact will make it easier for him to step back in. Family relationships matter, now and in the future. My mother-in-law and I became incredibly close during my husband's MLC. She's now "my mom." I could tell her all the stuff you really shouldn't say to anyone, but because he is her son—and we had done the work to understand what he was going through—I knew she wouldn't judge him or me for saying it. I know she loves him unconditionally, like I do. There are no words to describe how much she helped me on my darkest days.

I was very lucky because my husband told his parents, "It's me, it's not Amy." At first, he wasn't going to tell his parents when he moved out. But after a year of hell and lying to his mom about what was going on (I blamed my sad mood on my rheumatoid arthritis), I told him, "I can't tell your parents, you have to." Thank goodness he phrased it that way: "It's me, not Amy." While they initially didn't understand what was going on, they supported me through the entire crisis. The more I learned, the more I educated them, as well as my own family.

My sister-in-law is one of my best friends. I could tell her things that I couldn't tell just anyone. Plus, she had great insight. Again, I was very lucky in this regard. This is another one of the silver linings of MLC for me. Although we liked each other, we didn't really know each other. We both had been so busy taking care of our kids and we really only connected at family events. One day, she called me at her wits end about her youngest son. I believe she wanted to see if he could move in with us for a while. When she called, I listened, then I finally said, "Your brother moved out months ago." From then on, she became one of my best friends and supporters.

When I decided to move out of state, I felt I needed to tell his parents exactly why I was moving, that I was not bailing on our marriage, that I needed to get away from all the muck. I knew they wouldn't understand otherwise. I visited them for Thanksgiving. He was supposed to come too but backed out a few days before. His mom picked me up at the airport. His sister was at their house when I arrived. The hardest conversation I ever had with them was telling them why I was moving. I couldn't tell them that their son was having an affair with my best friend, someone they had met many times. My sister-in-law did it for me. I am forever grateful to her for that. She has been a constant source of support on my journey with Standing Spouses, and has celebrated every win with me, lifting me up during moments of doubt and reminding me why this work matters.

Friends and Neighbors

Friends and neighbors can be a tricky category for support. Some friends will disappear when your life gets messy. Some will be there for you, often not the ones you thought would be there. Some neighbors will gossip. Some people you thought were loyal will judge your choice to stand.

Tip:

- Share only what you must.
- Stay socially connected. Go to parties. Greet people as you pass them in the street but guard your heart.
- Don't make your husband's midlife crisis your entire identity.
- You need community, even if they don't get your story.

It's hard to tell anyone that your husband has decided to move out, and especially hard to share this with your friends and neighbors. As with your family and in-laws, here you are dealing with the same shame around what they might see as your failed marriage. In addition, you have to contend with the memories others have of fun times you and your husband shared with them. You might worry about how they will see you. Will they pity you? Will they judge you? Will they assume things about your marriage that aren't true? When you finally get up the nerve to tell them—because they wonder where his car has been the last few months—the reactions are often not what you would expect.

When I finally told my friends and neighbors that my husband moved out, they were initially shocked. The men unfriended him quickly, while the women stayed friends with him as they wanted to know all the details. "Is he with someone? I thought he was talking to her too much," and other such queries and comments. They quickly created their own stories and wanted to bad mouth him in front of me. Contrary to what they thought, bad mouthing his behavior didn't make me feel any better, only worse. He was still my husband, and I still cared about him, so hearing others criticize him was immensely hurtful to me, even if I was privately critical of him myself. For a long time, I defended my husband against the verbal attacks from friends, saying, "He's going through a rough time. He's lost. He'll figure it out." But eventually, I decided not to say anything because people who have never experienced an MLC will never understand.

Friends you thought were on your team, suddenly disappear, nowhere to be found. They don't like seeing you in pain and if you're not willing to "divorce his a$$" immediately, they don't stick around. The less said to neighbors and casual friends about MLC and your husband is best. You don't need to explain anything to them as chances are they won't understand it anyway. When your husband comes home, you don't want everyone to know all of your business.

That said, it is important to keep up neighborhood connections. Keep attending neighborhood parties and maintain conversations when you see neighbors on the street; otherwise, you end up in your own bubble. You need to be around people. I can't stress that enough. You don't have to talk about your husband with them, but you can't shut yourself up in your house and hide, even though that's what you want to do. It doesn't help you move forward in your life.

Both neighborhoods we lived in were important to me and my son during this time. Not everyone does things with their neighbors, but if you do, keep this connection. Community matters, even imperfect community. Why? Because connection matters. It's nice to be invited over for dinner or to sit around the fire enjoying a fall evening. It's also great to have people close by who look out for you, especially in emergencies. In one neighborhood, my son and I were trying to fix our shower head, and water was pouring downstairs through the garage ceiling. I had no idea where the water turn-off valve was. I ran to my neighbor, and he helped. Another time, after I moved, I was in severe abdominal pain. I drove myself to the hospital. It turned out to be appendicitis. When my neighbor learned of the emergency after I'd returned home, he chastised me and said, "Goddamit, Amy. Next time, call me!" It's really great to have neighbors like that.

The MLC Community

Finding other left behind spouses who understand MLC is critical. You need people who truly get it, not just those who sympathize, but those who understand. This is the community where you will find your people who know what you are going through. You can find them on social media sites like Facebook, but not all groups are alike. One word of caution: Some of the MLC groups are negative and all they do is complain. Some are all about male bashing, or many are stuck in victim mode and that's not helpful. Do not spend time in these groups. They will only suck the energy out of you. Stay away from the drama. Find the more positive groups that will support, educate, and cheer you on as you stand for your marriage and hold space for your husband as he comes to terms with his crisis.

I have a private Facebook Group for Standing Spouses. The tone of the group is very positive, with absolutely no negative vibes allowed. We are all about support, not about bashing our husbands. Not only do we have a growing group of like-minded members, but we also have coaches who know what you are going through and help respond to posts. Some are further along on the path of MLC and some have husbands who have returned home and are now out of the crisis. The coaches can mentor you and help you navigate all of the scary situations, like if your husband decides to file for divorce, the affair partner contacts you, or your children have a crisis in the midst of your husband's MLC. There is also a section featuring information for new members about MLC and recommended resources. To join the Standing Spouses Facebook Group, visit https://www.facebook.com/groups/standingspouses

Your Soul Sisters: LBS Friends

Within these spaces for left behind spouses, you will find your soul sisters. These aren't just online acquaintances. They become your lifeline. They're the women who text you every morning, who stay on the phone with you while you cry, and who cheer like crazy when you get even the smallest sign of progress from your husband.

I met my friend Jennifer in an online group the month my husband moved out. The group was more positive than most, and we clicked instantly. She became "my person." We texted every day, wished each other good morning and goodnight, and walked each other through the hardest moments. Her husband was further along in his crisis than mine was, so she could reassure me, "Oh, mine did that too. It gets better." And I was there to remind her of all the progress she has made, and how much progress her husband had made when she wasn't able to see it. She has done the same for me. Jennifer helped me start Standing Spouses. She's been my sounding board, my idea partner, and one of the biggest blessings to come out of this mess.

Then there's Grace, another beautiful connection made through these online groups. Her husband also came home, and he actually talks about his experience with her, which is rare. He often will share with her what he was thinking or not thinking during that time. Most husbands aren't able to give that kind of insight. Because of that, Grace offers a perspective few others can. She's not guessing; she's had real conversations with someone who went through it and came back. Her wisdom, support, and true friendship have been invaluable to me and many others. Grace is a fantastic mentor and friend who always knows what to say and how to put it. The MLC friends I have made are true friends who would do anything (and I mean anything) for me, and I would do the same for them. We have such a strong bond. Both Jennifer and Grace participate in my private groups and in my membership group, mentoring women going through MLC. You may feel alone now, but there are women out there who will become your circle, your family. You just haven't met them yet.

Coaches and Inspirational Mentors

Sometimes, the support you need doesn't come from friends or family, it comes from someone who has walked this road ahead of you and decided to light the way for others. Working with a coach who understands MLC can be life changing. I wouldn't have made it through my husband's MLC without the guidance of several key mentors: the incredible woman behind the name Hearts Blessing, Laurie from The Wife Expert, Cookie Rosenblum, and Brooke Castillo.

Hearts Blessing (she never disclosed her name) was the first person I learned from whose words made sense to me in the early stages of my husband's MLC. Although she never officially coached me, she helped me realize my husband was in MLC. She was my mentor in so many ways. Her website was my "ah ha" moment that he was in crisis. That was the first lifeline tossed into my storm. Her website was created more than a decade ago to help other spouses of MLC husbands understand the foundation of MLC. She was a true pioneer on this subject, and her work has impacted and saved many marriages and families. Hearts Blessing didn't just talk about MLC; she lived it, studied it, and devoted her life to helping others navigate it. Her wisdom grounded me when everything felt like it was falling apart.

Her work deeply shaped me. I wish I could have met her before she passed away, which happened before I began writing this book. She was a true angel. Her work has guided me on what to do, how to think, and how to hope. I never could have made it as a standing spouse without the incredibly insightful articles on her website. After her death, her family published a helpful book, *The Eight Stages of Midlife Crisis*, which explains the characteristics of what men go through during MLC and includes a compilation of some of the information on her website. Visit the website, read the articles, and please donate to Hearts Blessing if you find it useful. https://thestagesandlessonsofmidlife.org/sitemap/

Laurie, from The Wife Expert, helped me through an extremely difficult phase when I thought I might lose my mind with rage or grief or both. She taught me about kindness and compassion, and her humor, authenticity, and fierce belief in love grounded me. Her stories of husbands who come home gave me hope. Her videos were my Friday night dates, glass of wine in hand, when I needed someone to remind me that I wasn't crazy. Later, we hosted a retreat together at my house for twelve women where I finally met my best friends Jennifer and Grace in person. To learn more about Laurie's teachings and support, visit https://thewifeexpert.com.

Cookie Rosenblum was my first coach during this time. She taught me that my thoughts create my feelings. That one shift changed everything for me. She introduced me to the foundational concepts of thought work and helped me calm the anxiety, tame the fear, and manage my brain in a way that gave me my power back, even when everything felt out of control.

Later, I found Brooke Castillo, a highly acclaimed business and personal coach to thousands. She created The Life Coach School (LCS) and the Model, a clear, structured process for managing and working through your thoughts and feelings. Through her certification program, I deepened my understanding of her work and the Model and saw how this work could transform not only my life, but the lives of others too. Her framework made the mindset work click for me in a whole new way. It helped me connect the dots between what I'd learned and how to truly live it. Becoming certified as a life coach with LCS wasn't just a next step, it was the moment I realized that helping women navigate their husband's MLC wasn't just something I lived and survived, it was my calling.

These women didn't just *coach* me, they *changed* me. Now, through Standing Spouses and the Resilient Hearts program, I get to pass that support along to you. Learn more at https://www.standingspouses.com/resilient-hearts

Inspirational Authors

Books became part of my emotional support during this time. Reading the words of those who understand human transformation, resilience, and mindset gave me strength on the hardest days. I reread old favorites and discovered new voices that helped me keep going.

One of my favorite authors is Dr. Wayne Dyer. His work reinforced what I was learning through coaching: the power of thought, choice, and perspective. Here are just a few quotes by him that helped shape my mindset:

- "You cannot always control what goes on outside. But you can always control what goes on inside."
- "The highest form of ignorance is when you reject something you don't know anything about."
- "Be miserable. Or motivate yourself. Whatever has to be done, it's always your choice."
- "Your children will see what you're all about by what you live rather than what you say."
- "Conflict cannot survive without your participation."

- "With everything that has happened to you, you can either feel sorry for yourself or treat what has happened as a gift. Everything is either an opportunity to grow or an obstacle to keep you from growing. You get to choose."[24]

Each of these quotes reminded me of who I wanted to be, not just for myself, but for my kids, my future, and the legacy I hope to leave. I kept many of them on a digital Trello board, an online space where I could organize my thoughts, quotes, and insights so I could return to them again and again. Other authors I turned to included Martha Beck, Bob Proctor, Dr. Joe Dispenza, and Dr. Benjamin Hardy. Their wisdom helped me reframe this season of life not as a crisis, but as a transformation. Find authors who speak to your soul, whose words can sit beside you like a warm cup of tea when everything feels cold and uncertain.

You are the one person who won't leave you.

Don't Forget to Count Yourself

You may not feel it right now, but at the end of the day, your greatest support system is... you. That means learning to lean on yourself, not only out of necessity, but out of strength. So, don't forget to count yourself.

You may not feel like your own support right now. In fact, you may feel like the one falling apart. But here's the truth: You are the one person who won't leave you. You are the one who will be there at 2 a.m. when the world feels too heavy. That makes you powerful. It's not easy to feel strong when you're clinging to the side of the mountain, barely hanging on. But every climber has that moment when they want to give up and yet they find a way to keep going. That's what you will do. You might not feel powerful, but you are. Because you are here, you haven't let go. You're still climbing, still figuring this out. And that makes you strong.

This may be the first time in your life that you feel all alone, but you must have your own back. I know you're scared. I know you're not sure if your marriage is going to make it. You're embarrassed by your husband's actions and ashamed of your marriage. You're afraid of the future. That's normal. Be ok with feeling all these emotions. Don't stuff them down. See them for what they are: emotions. They can't hurt you. Just like a climber needs more than just a good grip, you're going to need more than just emotional awareness to reach the top of this mountain. You'll need your internal supplies of courage, determination, and commitment to find light, even on the darkest days. These are the tools you carry inside you, whether you feel them right now or not.

For this journey you're going to need to find your courage. Courage is acting in spite of fear. You hold space for your marriage, despite what anyone thinks. You also move forward in your life despite your husband's actions. Remember, this is a time for you to focus on yourself, to be honest and raw and open about who you really are, and then to love yourself anew. You aren't just surviving this; you are becoming stronger in ways you never thought possible. You are learning to trust yourself again, to make your own decisions without his input, and to stand firm when everything around you feels unsteady. Keep reminding yourself that you are enough, exactly the way you are. I'm sure you didn't know how tough you were until now and you're even more resilient than you know. In the Standing Spouses Membership Group, we have a saying: "We can do hard things." You're doing hard things.

Determination is another characteristic that is important as you stand for your marriage. You are not quitting on your marriage. You believe in the love that you both created through all of those years. You keep up your vows despite the fact that your husband seems to have forgotten them. That's what I had: fierce, gut-level determination to fight for what mattered most to me.

In the beginning, your mind is most likely fixated on one thing: saving your marriage. You just want him back. You want things back the way they were. But as you move through this journey, something shifts. You start to realize that the result you are fighting for isn't just about your husband returning, it's about you becoming the strongest, most grounded version of yourself in the process. You may not know this at first. In fact, I would bet you don't have a clue about that. But over time, you start to trust that whatever the outcome, you'll be ok, perhaps even better.

Commitment is the quiet force that keeps you standing, even when you're exhausted, uncertain, or tempted to give up. And let's be honest, you won't feel committed 100 percent of every day. Some days it might feel like zero percent. There will be moments when you want to walk away, when it all feels too heavy and you're just tired of it all. But on those days, when progress feels nonexistent, and hope is hanging by a thread, commitment is what brings you back to your why, your reason for standing. You remember the love you built, the life you shared, the vision you still hold.

Commitment doesn't mean you never waver; you will. And that is so normal. Wavering isn't weakness. Commitment is what helps you zoom out and look at the bigger picture. It's what helps you steady yourself, again and again. You're not just standing for him; you're standing for you. Part of that commitment to yourself means caring for your mind and your emotional well-being along the way. Because let's be honest, throughout this journey, your mind is on constant overload. You can't live in survival mode—uncertainty, fear, grief, and what if's—all the time. It's just too heavy. That's why you must be intentional about putting positivity into your life every single day.

Your survival brain will naturally spiral into negative thoughts, so it's your job to feed it something better. Positivity isn't optional here; it must be on your daily to-do list. Managing your thoughts is a full-time job, and it is challenging. So, don't beat yourself up in the beginning if all you seem to be doing is reframing your thoughts, such as shifting "Why is he doing this to me?" to "He's not doing this to me, he's not hurting me on purpose, he's doing it to himself. He's in MLC. This is what men in MLC do."

While you're doing the inner work, the outside world won't always understand. Most everyone thinks you are crazy for standing for your marriage. But you know deep down in your heart that the old husband you know and love is still there, barely recognizable at times, but you trust that eventually he will make his way back. Some days, that inner knowing roars because you see it in his actions. He sends a kind message, he remembers something meaningful, or he shows a flicker of the man he used to be. And other days? There's silence. Nothing. No text, no interaction, no hint that he even remembers who you are. Despite it all, you must have faith that everything will work out. This is where your MLC friends cheer you on. They know the significance of receiving a small text, a "like" on social media, a small connection in an online game or maybe even a TikTok from him. They know exactly what to say when the affair partner tags your husband or posts a picture with your husband on social media. They have your back. They remind you of your why for standing when you start to forget.

Your friends and your family don't walk in your shoes, so they really don't understand why you have chosen to stand. They might encourage you to move on, to protect yourself in ways that don't align with your heart. Their intentions may be good, but they don't always see the full picture of your journey. That's why you have to have your own back.

My original plan for this book was to prove that MLC is something deeper than a fling or the breakdown of a marriage. But the more I continue to research MLC and discover it is something deeper, the more I realize it doesn't matter what the outside world thinks.

What matters is what we, as standing spouses, think. I know there is something going on with my husband. He is not the same person I married and grew with for more than twenty years. He is struggling with something, and eventually, he will come out of it. I can wait for him to figure it out, but at the same time, I am working on myself and holding space for him. This doesn't mean becoming a doormat; it means loving him unconditionally despite his faults, figuring out my own failings, and hopefully coming together for a new marriage in the future. To quote my youngest son again, "Mom, as long as you believe, that's all that matters."

Before we wrap up, I want to make one thing crystal clear: You are the most important person on your support team. You are with you one hundred percent of the time. That makes you the most constant, important, and powerful part of this journey. Your inner voice, your resilience, your willingness to feel all the feelings and still keep going ... that is what carries you through when no one else shows up. So, celebrate the moments when you held your own hand, wiped your own tears, and whispered, "You've got this." You do.

Building your inner support system is critical, but remember, even with all the strength you're gathering inside, the outside world will still have something to say. Let's talk about how to handle the critics, and how to stop letting their opinions chart your path.

Contending with the Critics

A huge hurdle along this journey is dealing with everyone else's thoughts about it: friends, family, neighbors, and even strangers. Some will judge, some will pity, some will disappear. Almost all of them will have opinions about what you should do. But here's the truth: They don't get a vote.

One tool I learned on this journey came from Brooke Castillo, and it changed everything for me. It's called "The Manual." A manual is like an instruction book we write for other people, except we usually don't tell them about it. We expect our husband to act a certain way so we can feel better. We expect our friends to show up for us in a specific way. We expect our family to support us without judgment. And when they don't follow the invisible manual we created, we feel hurt, angry, and disappointed. The problem isn't just them, it's our expectations.

Your husband is not himself right now. He can't follow the manual you once had for him. And your friends? They may not know how to support you. Your family might be confused or uncomfortable. When you let go of the manual and focus on how *you* want to show up, everything shifts. What do you want the manual for yourself to look like? What kind of woman do you want to be during this time? Let that guide you instead of being guided by someone else's opinion or your old rulebook for how people "should" behave. When someone criticizes your choice to stand for your marriage, remind yourself: "They're reading from their manual, not mine." You don't have to defend or explain. You simply have to trust that your path is yours for a reason.

Let people be wrong about you. Let them think you're naive. Let them think you should be further along. Let them think you should have left by now. Let them be wrong. You're not living your life for them. You're climbing a mountain most people are too afraid to even approach. And someday, whether your husband comes home or not, you'll look back and say, "I did that. I stood when it would have been easier to run. I grew stronger instead of bitter. I scaled the damn mountain."

No Longer a "We"

You're in no man's land—not part of a couple, but not really single either. It's such an isolating and strange place to be. You don't belong in the world of couples anymore, though I've tried, and still try because I think it's important to keep connecting, even showing up at neighborhood parties where I'm the only single person in a sea of pairs. I also don't fit in with single women looking for new relationships, because dating is the last thing on my mind right now.

Oddly enough, I found more connection with widows, like my aunt who recently lost her husband. But even that's not quite right. Their loss is permanent, while there's still a chance my husband will return. Society treats widowhood as an acceptable kind of grief. People acknowledge the pain, offer support, and give you time to heal. But standing for your marriage while your husband is in MLC chaos is met with confusion, impatience, and outright judgment. People expect you to just move on, sign the divorce papers, and be done with it. There is no space given to grieve.

And grief is exactly what this is: the death of the old marriage, of the life you thought you had. Even if he comes home, what you rebuild will be something new and different. The old version is gone, and that loss deserves to be acknowledged.

The only people who truly get it are other left behind spouses. They understand the heartbreak, the uncertainty, and the resilience it takes to stand. Unfortunately, you meet most of them online and they do not live nearby, but thank goodness for Zoom, email, text, and late-night phone calls. Because when the rest of the world doesn't understand, we do.

What to Do Now

Now is not the time to go it alone. Find an online community for women in your situation. Check out my Standing Spouses Facebook page and join my free private community. A coach can help tremendously, so find one who is a good fit for you. Join my

Resilient Hearts program and learn how to manage your thoughts and feelings about this crisis and uncover how to create your best life. Sign up here: https://www.standingspouses.com/resilient-hearts

Get active. Start doing things with your neighbors and others, even if they don't understand what you're going through. Join in their activities. It's good to have support nearby. Having familiar people and a schedule of activities that feels familiar (even one that is new) helps you manage the day-to-day unpredictable nature of standing for your marriage. Learn to live with the uncertainty of the situation. Be comfortable with the uncomfortable and live in the now.

Make a list of your support system. Seeing it visually provides a mental anchor and helps you know who to call on for emotional support at a moment's notice.

Finally, read, read, read. Educate, motivate, and inspire yourself. Some of my inspirational favorites are Dr. Wayne Dyer, Martha Beck, Bob Proctor, and Dr. Benjamin Hardy.

Key Takeaways

- Find your own community.
- Your friends may not support you during this time. Make new ones.
- Find strength where you can from family, other left behind spouses, books, etc.
- Live in the present, be happy with the now; you can't wait until he comes back to be happy.

Chapter 7.

CRAWLING OUT OF THE HOLE OF DESPAIR: CLIMBING THE LADDER TO HEALING

Healing doesn't begin when the pain ends; it begins when you decide to climb, even while it still hurts.

~ Anonymous

Support helps, but eventually, the journey becomes solely an inner one. Building your support team is powerful, but even with people cheering you on, there will still be many moments when you feel deeply alone with your pain, many moments where you feel you won't be able to go on. That's not failure; it's part of the climb. Healing isn't just about reaching out to others; it's about finding the strength inside yourself to keep going when the path gets dark.

Somehow, recognizing and acknowledging that your husband is in MLC helps you feel a bit better about what has been happening in your life. Now, you know you aren't crazy; there's something to this. But getting started on your journey to survive the MLC and stand for your marriage is often the hardest part.

At first, it feels like you're trapped in a deep, dark hole. The light is faint, and the path upward seems impossible to climb. You're unsure of what to do, paralyzed by fear and uncertainty.

But there is a ladder out of that pit, a way to climb out. Even though it looks impossibly high, and the thought of taking that first step is terrifying, the climb is not only possible but transformative. The first rung is simply overcoming the fear of starting. Once you put your foot on it, you'll realize you're stronger than you think you are. With the right strategies, you can ascend from the darkness and emerge on the path to rebuilding your life with dignity and self-respect.

Top 10 Survival Techniques

These are my Top 10 Survival Techniques that I've learned from years of research, coaching, and personal experience.

1. Manage your mind
2. Name the story
3. Give him space
4. Avoid relationship talk
5. Watch for small signs he still cares
6. Practice active listening
7. Avoid complaining about anything
8. Find the humor and the absurdity in it all
9. Rely on your support system/safety net
10. Be the lighthouse

Let me guide you through each step of the climb so you can get on to the path to surviving this and creating your best self.

1. Manage Your Mind

When I learned to manage my mind, everything changed. It was like lighting up the dark hole I was in, and I could see more clearly. Immediately after bomb drop, my brain went crazy with all of the what ifs. *What if he moves out? What if we get divorced? What if I don't have money? What if I don't have health insurance? What if I don't have someone to spend the rest of my life with? What if he marries her (the affair partner)?* These are the thoughts that kept me up at night, kept me from eating, kept me from living my life. They paralyzed me. Looking back, I wasted too many years focused on worry and what ifs. Everything would turn out fine, but of course I didn't know that then.

Around that time, I started listening to Cookie Rosenblum's podcast, "Weight Loss Made Real." I was worried about my emotions and overeating. I had lost forty pounds a few years before and I didn't want to gain them back. Turns out, that was not a problem. Truthfully, I started listening to her podcast because it soothed me. Her voice was calming. It felt like she was there for me. And then, an amazing thing happened; I realized I wasn't listening to her for her weight loss advice. I was taking her advice on how to think about a situation. Soon, I used it to change my thoughts and alleviate my fears. Eventually, I joined her membership, and she coached me live. I credit Cookie with saving my life in so many ways.

As a result of Cookie teaching me about my thoughts, I went on to write a bestselling book during this time called *The Power of Food Prep*[25] and started a food prep membership group. My greatest takeaway from her lessons is that everything I think is not absolutely true. This was my light bulb moment, and it can be your floodlight in the darkness illuminating the ladder. By challenging your thoughts and reshaping them, you have the power to transform your entire life. Let me show you how. Choose to be fully present when you do the following exercise. You'll be amazed at how powerful your thoughts are and how they affect your emotions.

Make a list of everything that scares you. Don't freak out and go down that crazy road. You can't control any of that. It's just not good for your brain. Just write down all the fears and get them out of your brain.

My biggest fears were my what ifs:

- *What if he moves out?*
- *What if we get divorced?*
- *What if I don't have health insurance?*
- *What if I don't get a good paying job?*

Now, look at your list. How do you feel? I mean it; really think about it. Read it aloud and write down your feelings. Do you feel scared? Paralyzed? Anxious? Unable to breathe? What else do you feel? (I still feel panicked when I read this list, oddly enough).

Next, take those fears and what ifs and turn them around.

- *What if he doesn't move out?*
- *What if we don't get divorced?*
- *What if I have health insurance?*
- *What if I make lots of money?*
- *What if I do have someone to spend the rest of my life with?*
- *What if he doesn't marry the affair partner and he comes home?*

How do you feel now? Again, read those thoughts aloud and write down your feelings. What comes to mind? Do you feel a bit calmer? Not so crazy? Can you see how your thoughts create your feelings? This was my light bulb moment! Isn't this powerful?

> **Your feelings are never caused by him. They are always caused by your thoughts about him.**

You have control of your thoughts, and your thoughts are what create your feelings. Not everything you think is true. This one powerful realization saved my life: Your thoughts control your feelings. This is the floodlight in the dark hole. I survived my husband's MLC by learning to examine my thoughts, question if they were actually true, and intentionally change the thoughts that were pulling me down.

Here's a simple example of how thoughts can control your feelings: You might think, *My husband doesn't love me anymore.* Although it may seem like a fact, it is not. That is simply an opinion your brain is offering you based on fear and pain. Another common thought might be, *He's irritated and angry with me all the time.* Again, this is just a thought, not an objective truth. When you believe painful thoughts without questioning them, your feelings start to spiral in a negative direction. You might notice yourself feeling confused, insecure, unable to concentrate. You feel like you can't function anymore. But if you learn to challenge those thoughts—even just a little bit—you can change everything.

For example, maybe your husband actually does say, "I love you but I'm not in love with you anymore." (You know, the classic bomb drop.) Instead of beating yourself up thinking it's all your fault, you can choose to have a new thought: "That's what men in MLC say. He's following the MLC playbook. He is in MLC. He's depressed. Lots of men who go through MLC recover and resume a normal life with their spouse." Notice how that thought makes you feel— maybe calmer, more neutral, less like the world is crashing down on top of you. From that calmer place, you might start thinking, "My husband's MLC is not about me, but I can't wait on him, I need to live my life and let him do his thing. There's something I can do. I can work on myself. I will get through this and land on my feet, no matter what happens."

Your feelings are never caused by him. They are always caused by your thoughts about him. When you first learn to manage your thoughts, it can feel impossible to jump from total despair to complete confidence in one step. And that's ok. Healing your mind happens the same way you climb a mountain, one small steady step at a time.

This is where a tool called "thought laddering" comes in. I first learned about this concept from my coach Cookie and then more formally from Brooke Castillo at The Life Coach School. It changes the way you feel, one tiny step at a time. Instead of forcing yourself to believe something you're not quite ready for, gently move your thoughts up the ladder, starting from where you are right now, and slowly climbing to a better feeling place. Learning this skill has helped me through my husband's crisis, and it has changed how I approach everything in my life.

Every situation in life just is. It's not good or bad. You assign meaning to it with your thoughts. As Dr. Wayne Dyer said, "If you change the way you look at things, the things you look at change." This mental shift—understanding that I could change my experience by changing my thoughts—is the powerful floodlight in the dark hole. Let me show you how it works:

Sometimes, when you have a painful thought, like "I can't do this anymore," you try to change it, but your brain fights you. It's hard to go from that thought to thinking, "I'm creating my own happiness without him," but it's possible. Start with the thought that seems most believable, then work your way up to the more powerful, positive thought. This is how you gradually shift your beliefs one positive thought at a time.

1. "I can't do this without him."

2. "I've spent so many years with him at the center of my life, and I'm not sure where to start on my own."

3. "I'm realizing my happiness has always been mine to create, even if I didn't see it before."

4. "I'm learning to trust myself, find joy in my own life, and build something fulfilling just for me."

5. "I'm creating my own happiness without him."

Here's another longer example:

1. "He's never coming back."
2. "Right now, it feels like he's never coming back."
3. "A lot of MLC husbands say they are never coming back and yet still do."
4. "He's in MLC. His behavior is all about MLC. This is what they do."
5. "The affair partner isn't his magical soulmate, she's just a symptom, a distraction to the crisis."
6. "This infatuation/limerence phase won't last forever."
7. "Even if he doesn't realize it yet, the real problem isn't our marriage, it's his internal struggle."
8. "I don't have to fix him; I just need to focus on me."
9. "When he wakes up from this, he'll be looking for a safe, stable place. I can be that if I choose to."
10. "I don't know what the future holds, but I know I'll be ok no matter what."

Learning to manage your thoughts isn't about pretending you are fine when you're not. It's about choosing better thoughts to think, thoughts that keep you moving toward your goal of feeling better. Don't beat yourself up if you can't get there yet. This is a process, and it takes time. Climbing the thought ladder may be slow in the beginning, then feel messy and maybe impossible as you continue. But the more you practice, the more you take it one thought at a time, the stronger you will feel until one day, you'll wake up, and you'll have climbed to the top of the ladder and have emerged from the deep, dark hole. You will be more grounded, more you.

You don't have to believe everything all at once. You just have to pick a place to start and believe enough to take the next step. Before you know it, you'll look back and realize, "I didn't just survive this. I rebuilt myself in the process."

Even with all of the thought work and mind management you're doing during this time, expect your emotions to be all over the place. Learning to manage your thoughts is a twenty-four-hour job, especially in the beginning when you are new to it. So, hold on tight. Even though you may know it's not about you, it often feels like it is.

One minute, you hate your husband and wonder why in the world you are standing for your marriage. The next, you'll be crying your eyes out because you miss him so much. This is totally normal. It does get easier the longer the MLC goes on. Things that upset you, (usually about the affair partner), eventually don't bother you as much. The anger and judgment are there because he is not behaving the way you think he should behave. As soon as you stop being mad at him for not behaving the way you think he should behave and realize he is the only one in control of his behavior, you take back your power. You can't control your husband. You can only control yourself. When you try to control him and make things better, you only hurt yourself.

Part of managing your mind is coming to terms with what I call "living in limbo." This means you don't have to make a decision right now about your marriage. Our brain wants us to either fix the marriage or get divorced. Unfortunately, the brain doesn't like living in limbo and uncertainty. And MLC is uncertainty! Uncertainty means danger, and our survival brain hates danger, so it puts us on high alert to force us to take action.

But you don't have to know how this story ends yet. It's ok to live in limbo. You just have to use your evolved brain—the wiser, calmer part of you—that says, "I don't know what the future holds, but I will focus on today, one breath, one step at a time." Men in MLC don't know what they want. They can't make a decision right now. They are all over the place, so if you are standing for your marriage, you have to get comfortable with living in the uncomfortable.

During my husband's MLC, I realized that it was ok not to have all the answers. Learning to live in limbo is probably the hardest part of this crisis. While your survival brain wants you to fix everything right now, the real work is learning how to stay grounded in the present. (We'll talk about how to do that in the next chapter.) Gratitude helps with this.

2. Name the Story

Earlier I gave you an example of how your thoughts create your feelings and how changing those thoughts can change everything. But sometimes, your brain gets stuck. It loves to ruminate, obsessing about one thing and taking it all the way down the rabbit hole. Ruminating creates bigger fears and thoughts which lead to you feeling totally overwhelmed, out of control, and paralyzed.

Naming the story is another technique that helped me combat these overwhelming thoughts and fears. Here's how it works. When your brain starts off with "What if we get divorced?" and spirals into related thoughts, like "I'll lose my health insurance, I won't have any money, I'll be alone the rest of my life," etc., label the chain of thoughts as "The (husband's name) Leaves (your name) Story." Insert your husband's name and your name. For example: "The Ben Leaves Carrie Story." Naming the story gives your brain a way to recognize and dismiss those thoughts without having to think them all over again. Your brain loves to conserve energy, so it creates a rut and thinks the same thoughts over and over. When you name the story, you help your brain move on. It's like saying, "Yep, I got it brain. That's the ___story. We can move on now. We don't need to rehash and think all of those same thoughts yet again."

Another example could be that you tell yourself, "I'm not good enough. He left me for her because of _____." You could name that story "The (your name) feels sorry for herself story." It tells your brain "Stop it! We're moving on." It sounds so simple and maybe childish, but trust me, it works!

> ### *The key to connecting with him is having no expectations.*

3. Give Him Space

Your husband needs time to process his emotions. The best thing you can do right now is step back. This means:

- Avoid asking him for hugs or physical closeness right now. His nervous system is already overloaded, and your request—though completely natural—might feel like pressure to him. If it's appropriate, hug him, but don't ask. If he rebels against any physical contact, respect that. Eventually, his desire for contact returns, but don't push. If he hugs you, that's great. Give him a big hug back.

- Don't text, call, or email him first. Let him initiate contact when he's ready.

- If it's been a long time (at least a few weeks) since you last heard from him, you might try a connection text. I learned this from Lee Baucom's program. The purpose of this text is merely to let him know that you are willing to keep the lines of communication open. Do not text him from a needy or desperate place. This is a connection text. Make it pressure-free contact that does not require him to respond. It could be something as simple as: "Hope you're having a good day." or "Our daughter did the funniest thing today."

- Avoid questions like, "When are you coming home?" Practically any question you ask him will feel like pressure to him, and questions about his whereabouts or future plans are even worse. Most likely, he doesn't want to tell you about his life. Right now, he doesn't want to be responsible, and the family means responsibility. The affair partner represents freedom from all of that. Don't push. The key to connecting with him is having no expectations. This is very hard, but here's an example of what works: "We're opening presents on Christmas Eve. We would love to have you join us." Not, "You do plan to be there on Christmas Eve to open presents with the kids, don't you?" Or, try this: "Going to dinner tonight at Ben's favorite restaurant. Would love to have you there to celebrate his birthday." Instead of, "Are you coming to Ben's birthday party?" Do you see the difference? He may or may not show up but phrasing the request as an invitation rather than a question or a demand presents it as his choice instead of an act he's being pressured to do.

- Leave talk about work out of the conversation unless he brings it up, especially if he is mad about being the provider. However, if the subject does come up, thank him for working so hard and providing for the family.

Giving him space also helps you detach from all of your husband's drama. His drama weighs you down and holds you back. As desperate as you are to fix this, you can't; only he can.

When my husband told me he wanted to move out, it was devastating. I knew he was battling inner demons, and as much as I wanted to hold on, deep down, I understood he needed space to figure things out. I let him go, even giving him tulips and a note that said, "I hope you find what you're looking for, and I'll be here when you're ready to come back." I can't explain it, but I just knew he needed that from me (And that was before I had any coaching.). He was happy at first. He even invited me to his apartment, showed me all his new things, and we went out to dinner. He was like a little kid; it was so nice to see a flash of happiness in him. Unfortunately, that faded later because moving out didn't fix the problem. But I had to let him go.

Letting go and giving him space doesn't mean it stops hurting, but it does mean you're choosing to focus on your happiness rather than clinging to what you can't control.

4. Avoid Relationship Talk

As much as you want to have heartfelt conversations or drag him into couples therapy, don't. It's tempting, but it won't work right now. He's too consumed by his internal crisis to engage meaningfully. He doesn't know what's going on. He's not himself. He's the MLC husband right now. He may even say, "I'm never coming back." Don't believe it. So many of them say that. It's what they believe at the time. Others might say, "I don't want to give you false hope." I've talked to countless women whose husbands have said the very same things and have later come back. The "false hope" comment is another phrase straight out of the MLC Playbook.

For now, avoid all relationship talk:

- Don't beg or plead for him to stay; it only pushes him further away.

- Don't ask him to go to therapy. He won't listen, and he needs to arrive at that decision on his own.

- Don't label his behavior as a "midlife crisis." He won't believe you, and it could trigger defensiveness.

- Meet him where he is. My husband quit signing emails with "Love, (his name)." Instead, he would just put a dash. So, I started ending emails with "—Amy." The love is still there, but you can't push him to express it. Instead, focus on what you can control: your own actions and thoughts.

5. Watch for Small Signs He Still Cares

Even if he doesn't say, "I love you" anymore, he may still show it in subtle ways. Watch for small gestures, such as:

- Sending you a warning about a spam email.
- Fixing something around the house.
- Sending your parents texts or flowers on Mother's Day, Father's Day, etc.
- Sending you flowers on Mother's Day from "the cats."
- Bringing you his famous "smoked tri-tip" on your anniversary and acting like it was just leftovers, then saying, "Oh, I forgot it was our anniversary."

These little actions might seem insignificant, but they're a reminder that he still cares, even if he's unable to express it fully. Be sure to thank him for these little things. It means a lot to him. Thanking him changes his thoughts about you. Often during the MLC, he rewrites history and his perception to include negative thoughts. When you thank him, it disrupts this negative thinking about you. He does still care about you, otherwise he wouldn't pop in and do those things.

6. Practice Active Listening

When he does talk, focus on listening—really listening. Look him in the eye. Give him at least fifteen seconds before you respond. This may be hard to do, but it is so necessary. Don't interrupt him or offer solutions. Just listen. Avoid trying to fix his problems. Instead, respond with something like, "Whatever you think is best." This helps him feel respected and heard without judgment. If he's venting or monstering (acting out), stay calm and remove yourself from the situation if needed.

7. Avoid Complaining About Anything

He doesn't want to hear it. Even when you quit complaining, he still thinks you do so because that might be the story he's telling himself about you. Sometimes, it's such a deep rut engrained in his brain that it's hard for him to change his view or story of you. When you do make changes, he often doesn't notice them at first because he has come to expect certain behaviors from you. If you need his help with something like the garbage disposal, for example, tell him you have a problem and would like his advice on it. Tell him you want to "borrow" his brain. This goes over so much better than, "Can you fix the garbage disposal?"

8. Find the Humor and the Absurdity in it All

Humor helped me get through so much of my husband's MLC, especially sharing it with other left behind spouses. You can't be in it all the time. You have to look down at it and laugh at how absurd some of this stuff really is. My friends and I always say, "You can't make this s**t up!"

Some of the funniest things I discovered were from my son's girlfriend who stayed at my house for a month while the MLC was going on. She had a front row seat to the craziness because she often went to dinner with my son, my husband, and the affair partner. One day, while she was visiting, the affair partner pushed for them to go to dinner together. My kids were not fond of doing anything with her at the time, but they wanted to please their dad. My son's girlfriend came home and told me about the evening with her. I was rolling with laughter because apparently, my husband matter-of-factly mentioned me several times during the dinner in front of the affair partner. The affair partner was not pleased. My son's girlfriend said she had a mad look on her face every time he mentioned my name.

But the funniest story was when my husband came by to pick the kids up for another dinner, again with the affair partner who, unbeknownst to me, was waiting in the truck.

He came inside the house and said to me: "We're going to our favorite Chinese place. Do you want anything?"

Think of the irony here. "We," meaning the affair partner and kids, are going to "our," (mine and my husband's) favorite Chinese place. Then, asking me if I wanted him to bring me back anything? I was a bit dumbfounded, but I said, "Sure, get my favorite chicken. Thanks!"

Later that night, at dinner, my younger son ordered an extra portion of chicken. When my older son asked who the meal was for, my husband piped up and said, "Oh, that's for Amy." Can you imagine what the affair partner is thinking? *He's ordering food for his wife?* My son's girlfriend said the affair partner looked so pissed. After dinner, my husband dropped her off at her house on the way to my house with my dinner. He even stayed and talked to me while I ate it. You can't make this crap up. This is how I knew things were not right in his mind during the MLC.

One of my left behind friends said, "I don't know how any woman can stand to be in the shadow of someone's wife. And it's going to be like that forever. You can't erase twenty-five years. These women are idiots." And the men have no clue. They just do what they normally do, go where they normally go. I previously took offense because he had gone to our favorite restaurant, but thinking back on it, he really had no clue. He was too busy trying to survive. He didn't put any thought into anything. The kids wanted Chinese, so that's the place he chose to go. It could be a plus or minus depending on how you look at it. I chose not to take it personally and instead laughed at the stupidity of it. So, when you think his behavior is all about you, it's not. He does the same thing to the affair partner. He likes your posts on social media he also likes hers. He isn't thinking about anything except himself and what feels right at the time.

9. Rely on Your Support System/Safety Net

You cannot go through this alone. Find people who truly understand what you're going through, whether that's friends, family, or a community of women who've been in your shoes. They are your safety net.

Avoid advice from people who don't get it, especially divorced friends. Their experience is different from what you're trying to achieve. Their husbands may not have gone through MLC. Instead, seek guidance from trusted sources like older couples or an experienced MLC coach.

10. Be the Lighthouse

Last but not least, as you climb out of the hole of despair, ground yourself with an image of resilience and calm. Imagine being a lighthouse standing tall on the edge of a stormy sea. The waves crash around you, the winds howl, and yet you remain steady, a beacon of strength amidst the chaos.

Your husband's MLC is the storm. His emotions, decisions, and behaviors may feel erratic and overwhelming, but you don't have to be swept away by it all. Instead, focus on becoming the lighthouse: a source of light and stability, both for yourself and your family. But how do you do that?

Here is what being the lighthouse means:

- **Staying grounded:** Focus on your own emotional well-being instead of reacting to his every action. Let his chaos flow around you without pulling you under. Start a self-care routine: journaling, gratitude lists, and morning rituals can help you feel grounded. Be selective with your entertainment.

Avoid songs or shows that trigger negative thoughts that cause sadness, and instead, explore uplifting podcasts or hobbies.

- **Shining your light:** Reveal your calm, confident self, not to fix or rescue him, but to demonstrate that you are steady and capable of weathering the storm. Avoid excessive crying in front of him, especially the "ugly cry." Show him a version of you that is confident and thriving. Think about it from his perspective. Would you want to come back to a crying, depressed, lonely wife?

- **Standing tall:** Detach from his choices and focus on your own path forward. The lighthouse doesn't chase the ships, it simply guides them, standing firm. Now is the time to reclaim your joy and independence. As much as it hurts, don't wait for him to come back to start living your life. A happy, content woman is not only attractive, she is also resilient.

This mindset is especially important during moments when you feel tempted to engage in conflict, plead for answers, or fix what feels broken. Instead, remind yourself that you are the lighthouse. His storm is his own to navigate, and your role is to provide light, not to steer his ship. When the storm calms—and it will—you'll be proud of the strength you found to stand firm, even when it felt impossible. You are the lighthouse. You are the calm within the storm. And someday, when the skies clear, you'll realize you were always stronger than you knew.

There is so much more to this entire process of healing and mind management. If you're serious about changing your life, managing your thoughts about your husband's MLC, and deepening all of your relationships, I invite you to learn more with me. Visit my website: www.standingspouses.com and check out my coaching program. You will learn how to feel better and how to create your best life, all by managing your thoughts and emotions.

Learning all these strategies didn't just help me survive my husband's MLC, it changed everything about how I live my life. In fact, discovering this work is what prompted me to write this book and what eventually led me to pursue certification as a life coach with The Life Coach School. I originally learned the foundations of thought management from my coach, Cookie Rosenblum, and later discovered that the deeper model came from Brooke Castillo at The Life Coach School. I was so in love with the tools and the transformation that I took Brooke's certification course on Tools, completed her practicum, and became a Certified Life Coach, all so I could apply this life changing work specifically to the journey of Standing Spouses.

Over the past five years, I have pulled together everything I've learned to develop an entire program that helps women like you get through their husband's MLC, hold space for their marriage, and create a life they love no matter what the outcome. So much of surviving your husband's MLC comes down to mind management. What you tell yourself is everything. You choose your thoughts. Your thoughts create your feelings. And that changes your entire life.

Handling a husband in an MLC feels impossible at times, but it's about staying true to yourself while giving him the space to figure out his own path. His MLC isn't about you; it's a reflection of your husband's internal struggles. Focus on what you can control: your thoughts, actions, and happiness. Above all, remember this journey isn't only about him—it's about you becoming the best version of yourself. One practice that helped me become that woman was gratitude.

What to Do Now

Make a list of your fears. Think of the worst-case scenarios, then change them to the positive. Notice how your feelings about them change. Your thoughts are what you choose them to be. Your thoughts create your feelings, so choose your thoughts wisely. If you find yourself in a negative spiral, choose to read something positive, hang out with a friend, or do something else positive to get out of the negative.

Keep a journal of all of the funny things that happen. This will make you smile and laugh on the sad days. As you make progress in this area, reread this chapter. For more support, join my private Standing Spouses group on my website, StandingSpouses.com.

Finally, I often remind myself and my clients to stay on your own page. Live your life.

Key Takeaways

- Face your fears: "What if" doesn't have to be scary. We always go to the negative, it's our primal brain. Change the "what if" to the positive and see how you feel. Your thoughts create your feelings, so pay attention to your thoughts. Are they really true? How can you change them?

- Name the story when your brain decides to ruminate over the same thoughts.

- Give him space and let him be.

- Avoid relationship talk. This is not the time.

- Practice active listening.

- Find some humor in all of this. Humor is essential to surviving the craziness. It will help you, especially if you can tell your other left behind friends some of the crazy stories. Other friends won't get it.

- Rely on your support system.

- Be the lighthouse. I even bought a lantern to remind me. Maybe you want to find a symbol too: a little reminder that your light never goes out, no matter the storm.

Chapter 8.

THE COMPASS OF GRATITUDE: GUIDING YOU TOWARD PERSPECTIVE

Gratitude helps us to see what is there instead of what isn't.

~ M.J. Ryan

Learning to be grateful for everything, even the hardest, most painful things, has been one of the greatest silver linings to come from surviving my husband's MLC. I didn't realize how much I needed a big wakeup call on gratitude until life handed me one.

I am so grateful to have learned this lesson before my mom passed away. When she was diagnosed with terminal cancer, everything inside of me wanted to crumble. Instead of falling apart, I found myself doing something different; I slowed down and focused on living in the present. I treasured every moment I had left with her, and I was so deeply and fiercely grateful for everything she had done for me. The morning she passed away, I lay next to her and said, "Thank you for being a great mom. I love you." Honestly, without my husband's MLC, without the emotional work it forced me to do, I might not have been able to say those words at all. I might have been too wrapped up in my own suffering to see her and savor that sacred time together. I would never have learned the true value of gratitude.

I am also so incredibly grateful for my husband's extra financial support during this time as well. Because of his help, I was able to visit my mom almost every month for a year and a half, spending precious, irreplaceable time with her at the end. I thanked him for that many times, but there are no words big enough to express how much that meant to me (and to her).

If you're in the thick of your husband's MLC, you might be thinking, "Gratitude? Are you serious right now? I can barely breathe, and you're telling me I should be grateful during this time? And please don't tell me to write in a gratitude journal. You've got to be kidding!" I get it. It may seem ludicrous in the beginning but let me show you why this makes absolute sense during your husband's MLC. Hear me out, because gratitude is not about pretending everything is ok, it's about finding the light in the darkness. The more you practice it, the more you'll see gratitude isn't just a nice idea, it's a survival tool. Let me show you why it works for you. Trust me on this.

First of all, let's define gratitude for our purposes in this book. Gratitude is the practice of noticing and appreciating what's good, even when everything else isn't. It doesn't mean pretending everything is fine or ignoring what is hard. Being in gratitude means making space to recognize what's working in your life, what feels supportive, or even what brings a tiny spark of comfort or joy, even in the middle of this MLC mess. Gratitude is how you stay grounded in the good, without denying what you're going through.

So, why should you practice gratitude, especially now, in the middle of this storm? Because science shows it can literally change how your brain works and help you cope better. I've taken some key insights from this blog post on calm.com titled "The Science of Gratitude and How It Can Affect the Brain"[26] as well as some great information from The Neuroscience of Gratitude,[27] and added in teachings from Dr. Joe Dispenza,[28] who explains that gratitude is one of the most powerful elevated emotions for rewiring the brain. I've applied these concepts directly to what you're going through with your husband's MLC. Here's what you should know:

Gratitude can help build happiness into your life. When you feel genuinely thankful, your brain releases dopamine and serotonin. These are the happy chemicals that boost your mood and emotional well-being. The more you practice gratitude, the stronger these pathways in the brain become. You really need this mood boost right now because you are emotionally exhausted, heartbroken, and just trying to hold it together. Practicing gratitude won't erase the pain, but it can help you find those little pockets of light while you're fighting your way through the dark. They are like vitamins for the soul.

Gratitude helps regulate stress. When you're living with this daily stress and unpredictability, your body is constantly flooded with cortisol. Gratitude may help lower your levels, helping you feel calmer and more emotionally balanced. It helps your brain handle stress better, and when you're in survival mode, even a little bit of calm can go a long way.

Gratitude rewires your mindset. Gratitude helps shift your focus from what's missing and broken in your life to what is actually working, even if it's a tiny moment, like petting your cat and hearing her purr, or a nice hot cup of tea in your favorite cup that makes you feel human for just a few minutes. Over time, this practice retrains your brain to look for the positive instead of automatically spiraling into the thoughts of doom. When your husband is distant, absent, or making choices that break your heart, it's easy to fall into the negative loop of, "This will never get better." But when you practice gratitude, that loop gets interrupted by focusing on something in the present moment.

Gratitude boosts decision-making and empathy. Gratitude activates the prefrontal cortex, the part of your brain that is responsible for making good decisions, maintaining emotional control, and connecting with others. Being grateful can actually help you think more clearly and feel more connected. This comes in handy when you're faced with a monstering situation where you want to lash out at him. With the help of gratitude, you're more likely to respond from a place of grounded strength. Gratitude gives your prefrontal cortex the support it needs so you can make better decisions, have more empathy for yourself and him, and avoid getting caught up in his crisis.

So, what does all of this have to do with surviving your husband's MLC? Everything. Because when gratitude activates the decision-making, emotionally regulated part of your brain, it gives you the space to pause and to choose a grounded response instead of reacting from fear, resentment, or overwhelm. That pause is where your real power lives. It's the beginning of changing how you show up in your relationship, even if he hasn't changed yet.

Gratitude Isn't Always a Two-Way Street

People love to be appreciated. It doesn't matter whether the appreciation comes from a stranger or a loved one. Being acknowledged for doing or saying something that positively impacted someone else goes a long way to boost our joy and confidence, decrease negative emotions, correct misunderstandings, and interrupt potential confrontations.

Unfortunately, as women, mothers, daughters, wives, and female coworkers, we don't receive expressions of gratitude as much as we would like. We give, but we don't always receive, and that teaches us that gratitude doesn't aways work both ways. That can be frustrating. Because of this, we may not always express our gratitude to those we love and appreciate. After all, we do a lot that goes unnoticed or unacknowledged, so why should we go out of our way to express gratitude to others for doing what's expected of them? We might think, "They don't acknowledge or thank me for doing what needs to be done; why should I thank them?" If you use this logic when dealing with your MLC husband, changing your perspective can make a huge difference in how he relates to you.

During this time, you should go out of your way to express gratitude to your husband. This doesn't mean you should shower him with insincere compliments or praise him for merely being alive. It means is that you can use this time to step back and see the little things he does and says, and acknowledge him for doing so, even if he is doing the very least you expect of him as a man, a husband, and a human being. Right now, he needs all the positive feedback from you that you can give. When you start expressing thanks for all of the little things he does, it starts to make a difference in how he views you and your marriage.

Neuroscience actually shows us why this appreciation matters. When we are thanked by someone, or even when we witness gratitude in others, our prefrontal cortex lights up, activating the brain's reward circuits. This activation helps rewire our thought patterns and promotes positive change. In simple terms, being open to receiving gratitude allows us to recognize it as genuine and impacts us in a meaningful way.[29]

One time when my husband was unloading the dishwasher, I thought, *I could thank him. But I unload the dishwasher three times a day and no one ever thanks me.* Looking back, that was a huge mistake. As I matured during his MLC, I changed my approach and began to acknowledge my husband for even the slightest things he did, like stopping by to check on me, driving me to a doctor's appointment, or replacing the sprinkler head. This change in my perspective taught me that being grateful for my husband, and expressing it, caused him to want to do more things for me. It became a beautiful reciprocal thing, more like a two-way street.

After your husband moves out, you realize just how much he did for you. Some left behind spouses might need to be stripped down to their bare bones before they can be truly grateful for their husband. Unfortunately, that is what the MLC does to your relationship. Before, you might have complained that you did it all and you pointed out when he didn't carry his load in helping out around the house or with the kids. Once he moved out, you became grateful for every text, every visit, and every nice thing he did. Most likely, he'll notice the shift in your expression of gratitude for him, and deep down, he begins to feel more appreciated, useful, and wanted. If you haven't yet begun to show gratitude for your husband, now is the time. It's never too late to be grateful. At first, it might not be well received if he isn't used to hearing it, but eventually, he will start mirroring you and thanking you in return.

After my husband moved out, I started a gratitude journal. I first learned about the practice from author Bob Proctor,[30] and it was reinforced by my coach Laurie and others. At first, I had trouble finding things to be grateful for because I was so focused on feeling sorry for myself and my situation. I didn't feel like I was grateful for anything. In the beginning, all I could think of to be grateful for were small things, like "I'm grateful for my cats," because they were there to comfort me when I was so down. Soon, I expanded my list to bigger things: "I am so happy and grateful my husband is a great provider. I am so happy and grateful for my beautiful home." Now, I find at least ten things I'm grateful for each day. I also list three people who are bothering me in my life right now and send love to them. Those two practices have made a huge difference in my life. I notice that it has also rubbed off on my youngest son. He now thanks me for everything.

There is a fabulous book called *The Attitudes of Gratitude* by M. J. Ryan. Whenever I'm having a down moment, I pick up that book and read a few chapters. My copy is dog-eared and marked up with highlighter and has lots of colored flags. This gratitude book gets me back on track with my life. Gratitude impacts everything. While we are at it, thank you so much for buying this book. It means a lot to me. My goal is to help other women who are going through MLC, and you have supported that goal. Thank you from the bottom of my heart!

It may sound strange, but I truly am grateful for my husband's MLC. His crisis has taught me so many things and I have learned to handle so much on my own. While I wish I could have grown in a different way, I am a much stronger person now. That is another silver lining. You too will learn this. It's amazing all the things we can acheive when we don't have a choice. I know that might sound impossible to believe right now, but it's true. You will grow from this.

The Mountains I Have Climbed

As you probably already know, the rest of your life doesn't stop simply because your husband is having an MLC. Life goes on, and the same things that would normally happen still do. When you add MLC to the mix, it seems that any challenging life experiences are amplified. But as you become stronger and better through your MLC experience, you will discover a strength in yourself you didn't know existed. Just like I did. In fact, I faced so many things I didn't know I could handle until I had to. I list them here only to show you these were all the things I didn't know I could handle on my own until I was forced to do it.

There is a country song called, "Heart Like a Truck" by Lainey Wilson that came out during my husband's MLC. Every time I hear that song, I think of how strong I have become and how much I handled during these tough years. Although I know many women have dealt with so much more, these are some of the things I have endured during this period in my life. Interestingly, my husband has been there for me, in some small way, for everything. (You must look for the silver linings.) I am truly grateful for all of them. They all taught me something.

Health issues. I have rheumatoid arthritis (RA), but it had been in remission for ten years. Right after bomb drop, my body literally went into shock, and my RA got so bad that I could barely walk or use my hands. I am very grateful that my husband chose not to move out until I could get it under control again with the right medications. It took almost a full year to do that. My RA flares up in times of major stress in my life. Navigating my condition alone taught me about self-care and mitigating stress.

Six months after my husband moved out, I was diagnosed with melanoma on my face. It started out as a small freckle that later became a larger discoloration. My aunt insisted that I get it checked out. When I consulted a dermatologist, he didn't think it was anything, and then he saw the biopsy results. He was shocked when he called to tell me the news. "Amy, I'm so sorry, this is not what I expected. You have melanoma and you need to have surgery immediately." When my husband insisted on driving me to the surgery appointment, I was shocked. His reaction was: "Why wouldn't I take you?" I wanted to respond, "Uh, because you don't live with me anymore." After the surgery my husband brought me home and tucked me into bed. He came back later that night to check on me, then he disappeared for a few days. Thankfully, my youngest was there to help me.

My husband came back to help change the bandages a few days later. I just couldn't do it on my own. I remember seeing my face in the mirror, thinking how ugly it was. There was a scar from my eye all the way down to my jawline. I looked like Frankenstein. He was very tender as he took off the bandages and stroked my face. Tears rolled down my face. I felt so broken. That was one of my lowest points during this whole MLC. I discovered later he went on a trip with the affair partner during his disappearance. Thankfully, I didn't know about it then. Having a huge bandage on my face and later having to show my scar without makeup for months made me accept myself for me. The lesson I learned was not to care about what other people thought of me.

Hurricane Ian. My parents and sister live in Florida. For this hurricane, they decided not to leave and instead hunker down and wait it out. I didn't hear from them for four days as the power, internet, and cell service was out. It was horrible not knowing whether they were alive or not. It was then that I truly learned the lesson of letting go. I have no control over anything except myself. My husband was a great support during that time. He went on Twitter (X) and found every news story that he could find about their area to help keep me informed.

Aunt's death. The aunt who gave me Granny's ring passed away during my husband's MLC. She was one of my cheerleaders and my mom's best friend. This taught me the value of telling people how much they mean to you, in the moment.

Son's wedding. I was so worried about how my son's wedding would go since my husband would be there along with all of the family. I wasn't worried about my interaction with him because we were fine. But I wasn't sure how my dad and uncle would handle having him there. Thankfully, it was like old times. My husband was a gracious host, drove everyone around, and even danced with me at the wedding. This wedding taught me that family is family. And family is all that matters.

Uncle's death. My uncle passed away three weeks after the wedding. I am so grateful and blessed that my uncle was able to attend, and even dance using his walker. It was a huge deal for him and my aunt to attend. It was a special time for everyone. They drove two days to get there. The day they returned home, my uncle fell. He passed away a few weeks later. My husband was there for me, again in his small MLC way. He sent flowers and texts to my aunt as well.

Moving to a new state. Although leaving the proximity of your spouse is not recommended, I had to. If at all possible, you should try to remain in the home during your husband's MLC. Eventually, they return and hope to find home. Your home is the lighthouse. However, in my case, I couldn't stand living there. The affair partner lived near us. I would frequently end up behind her at a stoplight. Each day that I drove past her turn-off was excruciating for me. So, I decided to move to another state, one I had visited with my husband. We both liked it, and some of my husband's relatives lived there. Moving was probably the best thing I could have done for myself. Building a brand-new house on my own, then meeting new neighbors, and starting a new life was exciting. Doing it without much help from my husband was a liberating and powerful act. I am so grateful my youngest son came with me. He'll never know how much that meant to me.

Solo travel. One of the scariest moments happened when I was driving back from my uncle's funeral alone. It was a long drive, almost 3,000 miles round trip. During the drive, the pressure of one of my tires dropped. I was alarmed, so I called my husband. He was very concerned, but he couldn't do anything about it. He told me to put air in the tire and that it would probably be fine. I ended up with a very low tire in the middle of nowhere. I was scared to death. This is where being grateful and relying on the goodness of humanity came in.

I pulled into a gas station, but they didn't have air. They didn't even have a bathroom. The clerk was so nice, she went and got her boss who drove home, got his air compressor, came back, and pumped my tire enough to drive to the nearest town, forty-five minutes away. He wouldn't take any money and said, "I live for this stuff." I will forever be grateful to him and Wickel Tire Pros. They got me right in, took the big nail out of my tire, and didn't even charge me. People are so kind.

Mom's cancer. This one was a biggie. When I got the news of my mom's cancer diagnosis, I was so distraught that I couldn't think of anything else except to call my husband. He answered immediately, as I never called him. I nearly choked on the words, "Mom has cancer." This one was the hardest thing to deal with on my own. My husband was my rock, my support, and not having him every step of the way was so hard. But I am grateful that he was there when I called him. When my mom was first diagnosed, I flew to Florida every month for almost a year while she did chemo. He even gave me extra money to do this. Looking back, I believe that my husband's MLC prepared me to accept her cancer. It taught me how to live in the now, treasure the present, and not worry about the future. It also taught me that my problems were small in comparison.

Mom's death. I am so grateful my husband was there for me during this time. I tried not to call him too often, but when I did, he was there for me. He even told me to call him anytime, which is rare for an MLCer. He attended her celebration of life and stayed all weekend helping out. Later, he told me he had a really good time with everyone.

I mention my struggles so that you can see that I survived some of life's most difficult moments even in the midst of my husband's MLC with him there to support me. Even after he had moved out, I could still count on him in small ways. When I look at the list of so many (but not all) the things I went through during this time, I think to myself, *Wow! I am pretty fricking amazing!* These experiences helped make me who I am today. While I wish I could have gone through this transformation less painfully, I am grateful for it.

Although my husband wasn't there for me during these crises in the same way he would have been normally, I am amazed that he showed up in the small ways that he did, despite being in the midst of his MLC. I learned to look for, appreciate, and be grateful for these small but steady moments. This is why I know in my heart the love is still there. He has been there for me in the best way he knew how during everything he was going through. We have a connection and a bond that is still strong. It may not be the outpouring it once was, but it's still there.

What Does All This Mean for You?

Those were some of the mountains I had to climb. You will have yours. The main thing to remember is to be grateful in the moment for what you have, even if it's small, because those small things add up. When you are grateful, you live in the present. Focusing on the present grounds you and makes all of the other distractions in your life minimal. Focus on what you have right now, at this moment. This is really one of the keys to surviving this crisis.

Look for the little things that your husband does. You may be angry about his relationship with the affair partner, and feel ignored and pushed aside, but pay attention to those little things he does to show you he still cares. Though they may seem small, they are tiny gems that show you that the man you fell in love with years ago is still in there. However, you must foster kindness to him first. The kindness and gratitude you show to him will go a long way. He will mirror it back to you, but you might have to sort through all of the rocks to find it.

Two sayings that have stayed with me.

The first is from a quote I once saw on Facebook, simply credited to someone named Luis: "When someone helps you when they're struggling too, that's not help, that's love."

The second came from Jennifer, a fellow standing spouse and dear friend: "They bury their love for you under their depression." That love—however buried or hidden—still finds a way to peek through in the small, unexpected moments. And when it does, it reminds you that you're not crazy for holding onto what was real.

Gratitude became the ladder that helped me start climbing out of the darkness. But make no mistake, there were days when even gratitude didn't feel like enough. In the next chapter, I'll share what it felt like to hit rock bottom, and how I started to claw my way out, one tiny, shaky step at a time.

What to Do Now

When you are grateful, you are focused on receiving from others. Write a list of ten things you are grateful for every day. Send love to three people who bother, annoy, or irritate you. This practice alone will change your life.

Start thanking and being grateful for all the little things that your husband does now (you may have never noticed them before). The little things eventually turn into bigger things, and that gives you hope that the husband you married is still in there. So, if he comes by and fixes the toilet, make a big deal about it and thank him. When you interact with him, express your gratitude for all he has done for you. He may be standoffish at first, but eventually he will mirror it back to you.

Get a copy of *Attitudes of Gratitude*. Read a chapter before bed, when you wake up, and when you feel very negative. It really helps!

Key Takeaways

- Some of the scientific benefits to being grateful include a better mood, greater happiness, stress regulation, and rewiring your brain.
- Being grateful puts you in the present.
- Getting through your husband's MLC makes you a stronger woman.
- You don't know what you can do until you're faced with challenges.

Chapter 9.

CROSSING THE RAVINE: HOW TO GET THROUGH THIS CRISIS WITHOUT LOSING YOUR MIND

Rock bottom became the solid foundation on which I rebuilt my life.

~ J.K. Rowling

*E*ven with all of the gratitude work I was doing, there were still days when it felt like the weight of the world was crushing down upon me. Gratitude helped shift my perspective, but it didn't erase the pain. And there were moments—raw, gut-wrenching moments—when I didn't know how I was going to survive.

After my melanoma surgery, I felt completely invisible to my husband, and to the world. Although he had come over to help remove the bandages from my face after the surgery, he'd disappeared for days after that, leaving me feeling broken and beaten down. Early one Sunday morning around 2 a.m., a few days after the bandages were removed, I got up, put on my robe, and shuffled into the bathroom. When I caught a glimpse of myself in the big mirror—my face still swollen, still stitched up like Frankenstein—I barely recognized the woman staring back at me. My face was so ugly, so broken, so damaged. It looked the way I felt. That's when the dam broke. I sank to the cold tile floor and cried like my heart was breaking into a million pieces, because it was. I wanted him to come save me. I wanted him to make it all better. This was my lowest point in all of this crisis.

I lay there in that dark moment on the bathroom floor for what seemed like hours. Finally, the thought came to me: *When I get through this, when I get to a better place emotionally and mentally, I'm going to help other women going through this. No one should ever have to survive this alone. Not ever.*

That morning on the bathroom floor didn't magically fix everything, but it was a turning point, a quiet decision that somehow, some way, I would keep going. I knew I couldn't stay stuck there forever. I had to find small ways to pull myself out of the darkness, even if it was just one small shaky step at a time. At that point, I knew, I was the only one who could save me.

Practical Steps for Moving Forward

He can't save you; only you can save you. I know you want him to come back, to say he's sorry for all the dumb crap he did, to say he wants only you, to beg forgiveness, to be the man you want him to be. That's what we all want. But that's not what we need. The truth is: You don't need anyone to save you. You have to have your own back. I had to learn that, and so do you. When you're standing at rock bottom, it's not about finding that quick fix, it's about stacking small wins, tiny actions that slowly build your strength, one piece at a time.

Here are some of the steps that helped me start crawling out of that dark place:

Write it out. In the beginning, when I couldn't tell anyone about what I was going through, I would write or draft emails to him that, of course, I did not send. I would just get it all out, furiously typing at my keyboard. "How could you do this to me?" "Why didn't you ever take me there?" "Why don't you want to spend Christmas with us?" "How could you just throw away 25 years?" "Why are you with her?" "Don't you care about our family?" I poured out all of my anger, hurt, and confusion. It was cathartic. Whether it's drafting emails you never send or jotting in a notebook, let it all out. These are just your thoughts and feelings. They won't hurt you if you process them.

Download your thoughts. Write out your thoughts on paper and describe how you feel. We spend so much time avoiding negative feelings when what we really need to do is sit down, write them out, and actually feel them. Those feelings usually last less than a few minutes. After you acknowledge your thoughts and the related feelings, reflect on them. Are they facts or stories you tell yourself? Separate fiction from reality. This practice, combined with coaching and supportive communities like the Standing Spouses group, can shift your perspective and provide relief.

Embrace the concept of 50/50. Here's a newsflash: We aren't meant to be happy 100 percent of the time. I first learned this from my coach, Cookie. Somehow, I had come to believe that I should strive for happiness at all times. Cookie said, "Most people experience happiness about 75 percent of the time." Another one of my coaches, Brooke Castillo, says it's even less than that, about 50 percent. When you release unrealistically high expectations of yourself, you also relieve the pressure to be happy all of the time. When you realize it's normal to be 50/50 or 75/25, you begin to understand that if you have a down day or a bad moment, it's ok. But remember, you are the only one in control of your happiness. You may think your husband did this to you, but that is just a thought about the situation. You are not in control of the event, but you are in control of your thoughts and feelings about it.

Have your pity party. If you need to have a daily pity party for yourself, go ahead, it's ok; just keep it brief. Set a timer so you don't go over fifteen minutes. At some point, you need to pick yourself up and figure out what you are going to do with your day. In the beginning, you may need to set the timer multiple times a day. Be kind to yourself. This is hard.

Remind yourself that life doesn't suck. Use inspiration calendars, affirmation cards, or uplifting quotes to remind yourself of the good things in each day. Bob Proctor's daily quotes saved me more times than I can count. To support my clients, I created "3 Minutes to Thriving," a daily video series designed to uplift left behind spouses. It's part of my membership, and it can be purchased separately at www.standingspouses.com.

Make lists. In the beginning, when you might still feel depressed and confused about MLC, your brain is stuck, and you might feel inept to do even the simplest things. In this case, rely on the power of lists. I started making simple lists of things I needed to do, such as brush my teeth, make my bed, eat something, or take out the trash. It may sound dumb, but when you're depressed, you need a list to get anything done. If it was on the list, I did it. The list helped keep me busy, gave me purpose, and made me feel like I accomplished something. It is gratifying to cross things off the list after completion. As time went on, my lists became less about simple daily tasks, and more complex with a focus on business. But those early lists really helped me. Eventually, the focus of your lists evolves from picking yourself up emotionally to working on your goals and dreams. Don't beat yourself up if you don't tackle those goals and dreams right away. It takes time. Give yourself some grace.

My friend Jennifer made lists as well. Hers included lists with titles like:

- Why I love him (pre-MLC).

- Why I respect him (pre-MLC).

- What I know vs. what he says (since they say a lot of nonsense that never actually happens).

- Why I am a badass (we need to shore up our beaten self-confidence).

She explained all of this in one of our workshops: "These lists are crucial to reframing your thoughts and opening your mind to kindness, assuming you want to move forward with kindness and find empathy. Empathy is the way forward with you thriving no matter what. Holding on to anger and hurt will leave you bitter and stuck."

Shifting Your Perspective

One thing you can do during your husband's MLC is learn how to see your situation differently. This doesn't mean sugarcoating what is happening; it means choosing to respond from intention instead of reactivity.

Here are some practical ways you can shift your thinking: planning ahead for emotional triggers like holidays, learning to detach with love, staying focused on your own growth, building new routines, and even beginning to reframe this painful season as an unexpected gift. These shifts won't make the pain disappear, but they will help you navigate this with more peace, clarity, and strength.

Have a plan for special occasions. Make plans for holidays, vacations, weekends, and even quiet Friday nights. Whether it's going out or staying in to watch a movie, having something on the calendar gives you a sense of control and purpose. Don't spend holidays, anniversaries, or special occasions alone unless you've got a clear plan for how you'll handle them.

Holidays can be especially tough, but planning ahead is essential to your emotional survival. Consider visiting his family. After my husband moved out, I made a point to visit his family for Mother's Day and Thanksgiving. I even invited them to visit me. For Christmas, I went to see my own family. Taking these trips can be restoring to the soul but be prepared; it can get emotionally heavy if you don't manage your thoughts beforehand. Family members often ask questions, expecting answers you simply don't have. I've found that redirecting the conversation and gently educating them about MLC works best. Over time, they begin to understand.

Detach with love. This is a critical skill you need to learn in dealing with your husband's MLC: detach with love. Let him go! It may sound counterintuitive, but you must do this for your own sanity. You need to separate yourself from his actions and reactions, and that can be very challenging at times, especially if your husband is posting pictures of him and his new affair partner and tagging people in his new life on social media.

Learn to detach and live without him. Work on yourself and let the sadness and bitterness go. Get your ego out of it. This is not about you. Don't let his actions control your life and your happiness. You can't put your happiness on hold until he comes home. You have the right to be happy now, so don't try to save your happiness for when he comes home.

Learn to let go. Detach from him. Work on yourself.

This is where the thought work mentioned earlier is so critical to your well-being. If you don't detach, then you could end up suicidal or in a mental institution. In the beginning, most spouses react to their husband's actions while in MLC. "He did this to me! How could he do this? He doesn't love me!" Learning how to not react is key. "Stay on your own page" was a phrase I said often. Not letting the actions of others control your feelings is critical for your progress during this time. Similarly, allowing others to take full responsibility for their choices takes the burden of guilt and responsibility off you. This equates to you not fixing things and letting people work out their own messes. This is actually a great skill that you can apply to all areas of your life, including dealing with your kids.

When you detach from your husband, it doesn't mean you don't love him; it just means you are separating yourself from all of his drama. (Look at Hearts Blessing's Detachment posts). Detaching means you deal with your own issues and problems on your own; you don't call him, you don't text him, and you don't go running or crying to him. You don't rely on him anymore; you rely on yourself. This doesn't mean you don't speak to him; you definitely do. But you wait for him to reach out. When he does, and he will, you speak in a loving and grateful way. You thank him for the little things, even if they are tiny. You allow him to live the crazy life that he has chosen, and you live yours. It sounds so counterintuitive: In order to help your spouse, you actually don't help him. You separate from him and let him figure it out while you live your life. This is so hard, especially at the beginning. Eventually, you realize this is the best way to help indirectly. You let him ride his roller coaster life while you just watch from above without getting sucked into his drama.

Resisting detaching is a frequent mistake I see with my clients and in the left behind spouses groups. People who get so caught up in the drama of their husband's actions get drawn into the muck, which is not where you want to be. Stay out of the muck! Don't look at his social media. It's vital to separate yourself from him. Don't focus on his actions. You cannot control him. If you try to control him with angry threats or bad behavior, you only end up hurting yourself. Trying to argue with his reality and make him change doesn't work. Let go of your expectations of him. He is his own person.

You have to take care of you. Process your emotions. Allow yourself to grieve but also let him go. When you let him go and give up the expectations you have for him, you gain control of yourself and your emotions. Eventually, you learn that your life does not need to revolve around him, and that you are separate from him. You can't control him; you can only control yourself, your thoughts, and your actions. You may worry that the path of detachment leads to divorce. I reassure you that detachment is about your emotional health, not about the ending of your marriage.

Detaching comes in waves. Some days, you are really good at it and other days not so much. But it is very critical that you try to detach, especially in the early days of the crisis. At the beginning, he doesn't want to be with you, he blames you, he resents you for all of his problems. When you detach, he will eventually realize that you are not the problem; he is. Often, reaching this point takes a very long time.

Later in the MLC process, you start becoming friends with him again and he begins to reenter your life. Detachment transforms into connection. I am very grateful that my husband was farther along in the process when my mom received her diagnosis as I was able to talk to him about it. It wasn't the same support I would have received when we had a normal, loving marriage, but it was enough connection to where I felt supported.

I often reminded myself to, "Stay on your own page." Detaching from your husband also means staying on your own page. You're on this journey for a reason, too. Don't be the victim; it doesn't serve you at all. Life happens. Minister and author Michael Beckwith says, "It is what it is, harvest the good and forgive the rest." Take yourself out of the equation. Look down on it from above. He did not do this to you; he did this to himself. You cannot control him. This is not about you. This has nothing to do with you. And once you realize this, you can start to work on yourself and heal.

Maybe my husband comes home, maybe he doesn't. Maybe I will move forward with a new relationship. Rather than focusing on standing, I focus on the journey and give myself time to work on myself before moving on to a new relationship. I am a better person for the journey.

There is no single way to get through this. Ultimately, you will discover what works best for you. While some women decide to date or begin another relationship right away, allowing yourself time to process what is going on in your life is most often the best course of action. After all, no one else can make you happy besides you. Work on making yourself happy first before moving on to another relationship.

All of the strategies above helped to shape the person I am today: a much nicer, kinder, and more flexible version of myself. Having embraced so much of what I learned through my personal development resources, I don't complain as much, I don't try to control situations anymore. I have learned to live in the present, and to let go of expectations of others. While I wished I could have learned these things in a different way—rather than through my husband's MLC—I am grateful I learned these things about myself.

Building a New Routine

Building a new routine in my life is another strategy that helped me move forward. You need to change things up a bit; otherwise, you'll be tempted to go down a negative path of thoughts like, "We always had coffee together in the morning and now he's not here." When you build new routines in your life, it helps you manage the reality of him being gone.

Morning: Start a daily self-care routine. Write in your gratitude journal and do a thought download every morning. Subscribe to my "3 Minutes to Thriving" to get your day started on the right foot. Make it a ritual and look forward to having a cup of coffee or tea while you write in your journal.

When you focus on what you have, rather than what you don't have, you practice gratitude. This also helps you focus on the present and not on the future, which can look very scary. Write down ten things you are grateful for. As boring as this might sound, do it anyway. I do it daily, and I really feel grateful.

Exercise each day. This doesn't mean you wake up early every morning and go to the gym (although it can). Your exercise can be as simple as going for a walk. It doesn't matter what time of day, just make exercise a habit. If you can, fit some kind of movement into your schedule a few times a day. Whenever you find yourself angry, exercise! It helps clear your head.

Evening: Creating an evening routine can help you calm down for the night. Light your lantern to remind yourself that you are the lighthouse. Maybe take an evening walk or take a bath. Write in your gratitude journal, again, maybe just a few things about the day. Find something to be grateful for. Create a simple ten-minute routine that causes you to slow down and be present.

Pay attention to what you do before bed. The subconscious mind is powerful and will take your last waking thoughts into your sleep state. So, read something happy, positive, or uplifting before you fall asleep. Don't look at social media before bed. If you can't sleep, try listening to podcasts or watching meditation videos to take your mind off any negative thoughts. Fill your mind with good thoughts before you fall asleep. If you wake up in the middle of the night and can't sleep, get up and read or do some work. Don't lie in bed just thinking negative thoughts about what's happening in your life. Be productive, then lie down again when you're sleepy and try to fall asleep. The direction of your healing begins with your mental attitude. It either invites the light in or keeps you circling in the dark. As William Wordsworth said: "Your mind is a garden. Your thoughts are the seeds. The harvest can either be flowers or weeds." So, pay attention to your thoughts and what you are planting in your mind.

Weekly: Once a week, plan at least a few hours to yourself. Your "me time" can be anything, from leisurely reading to a spa day to dinner at your favorite restaurant. Have a friend, family member, or someone to watch the kids if you have younger ones.

Read: My weekly routine included curling up with a good book for a few hours on Sunday. I still do this, and I look forward to this sacred time. My goal throughout the MLC was to work on myself and become a better person, not for my husband, but for myself, so I could handle the hard stuff on my own and become the best version of myself. None of the books I read for self-care were about MLC; they were books on personal development. I read stacks of books during this time, taking notes, highlighting sections, and rereading anything that helped MLC make sense to me. Some of the things I learned from these books include how to let go, how to get your ego out of the way, how to stop being a people pleaser, how to stop being judgmental about others, how to not care what people think about you, and more effective ways to set and achieve new goals.

I also listened to dozens of podcasts. Books and podcasts were two of my most treasured resources. You will find your own resources. Each resource is a piece to the puzzle of your life, and everyone's puzzle is different. What works well for some may not work for you.

Start a Trello board: The best thing you can do for yourself in the early days is to educate yourself on MLC. Knowledge is power. Another essential step is organizing your thoughts about it. Create a Trello board to keep all your MLC information in one place. Trello is a free, simple online platform that is incredibly effective. I first began using it during my husband's MLC, and now I use it for everything from setting goals to managing business ideas.

Initially, I named my board "Motivational Quotes," a discreet title that kept its true purpose under wraps. One of the first things I added was a quote that resonated with me early in my journey. The quote didn't have a source, it was just a picture of a sticky note that said, "Dear Me, I know you are scared, but you can handle this. Love, Me." From there, I added notes about resources, reflections, self-improvement goals, strategies for managing my husband's moods, and "scripts" for what to say during difficult conversations with him. Even now, I rely on my Trello board because I organized it quite well in the beginning. It's searchable, so I can quickly find anything I've saved. It's been a lifesaver, and I'm confident it can help you too.

Reframing This Time as a Gift

Think of this time as a precious gift. At first, I saw it as a nightmare that I would never wake up from. But over time, I began to see it differently. This space, as painful as it was, became an opportunity to rediscover who I am and what truly makes me happy.

Use this time to create new dreams and goals for yourself, to stand on your own two feet again without your husband and mature into the best version of yourself. This growth parallels your husband's crisis, except your journey can be constructive rather than disruptive. By the time you two come through this, you'll be stronger individually and create a new and more resilient marriage.

There is no right way to climb this mountain; there is only your way. With every hard day you survive and every small choice you make to take care of yourself, you are climbing up the mountain to the next level. You didn't choose this mountain, but you do get to choose how you climb it. Some days you will slip. Some days you will soar. Just keep reaching for the next rock, the next ledge, the next small act of courage. Even the tiniest steps matter when you're climbing your way back to yourself.

Once you have created space in your mind, it's time to create space in your life, just for you. This is where my "Self-Restoration and Project You" begins.

What to Do Now

As you move through this process of personal development and growth, make a short list of three to five things you can accomplish today, even if it's just brush your teeth, eat lunch, and take a walk. Cross each item off as you go, then celebrate the small wins. You can also use lists to organize your thoughts, whether that includes tasks or your emotions about what's happening with your husband and marriage.

Doing a thought download to get the mental chaos out of your head and onto paper will work wonders for your mood and confidence. Don't censor, just write. With your list complete, ask yourself: "Is this a fact or a thought? What am I making this mean?" Set a timer and feel your feelings. If necessary (and sometime, this is really necessary), give yourself a fifteen-minute pity party.

Detach with love. This takes practice, but you can do it. Stop chasing, texting, explaining, or trying to fix him. This is your time to grow and shine! As you create a daily routine that grounds you, you will see consistent growth and power in yourself.

Key Takeaways

- Rock bottom can be the foundation of your healing if you let it to be.
- You don't need to fix everything today. Just take one small step.
- Emotions are not dangerous. Feeling them is how you move through them.

- Your thoughts, not your circumstances, create your experience. That means you hold the power.
- Detachment isn't rejection, it's love with boundaries and a lifeline for your sanity.
- You can live in limbo and still live a meaningful life.

Chapter 10.

HOW TO REACH THE SUMMIT:
SELF-RESTORATION AND PROJECT YOU

The most important relationship you will ever have is the one you have with yourself.

~ Brooke Castillo

During this upside down season in your life, there are two things that matter most, what I call the two non-negotiables: Self-Restoration and Project You. These are not optional; they are essential if you want to stay grounded and sane through this journey.

I have saved them for last. In the beginning, all you can do is focus on the crisis because you are in survival mode. Your whole world is crashing down around you and thinking about yourself feels impossible at the moment. But once you wrap your head around this, you will realize it's not selfish, it's self-preservation. You can't pour from a broken heart, but the sooner you start to focus on yourself, the faster you will heal and move forward. These two things will lift you up and out of this black hole. Trust me on this.

Self-Restoration

Many people call this self-care, but I like to call it self-restoration. That doesn't mean it's all bubble baths, scented candles, and soft music. Self-restoration is about figuring out your nonnegotiable needs and then making sure you consistently and regularly find a way to fill yourself up by taking care of those needs without feeling guilty. The key is to not feel guilty.

As women, we often feel guilty if we take care of ourselves first. Try to think of these self-care activities as things that charge your batteries. If your batteries are depleted, you can't be happy and enjoy your life. Your mood and your attitude trickle down to everyone in the family. If mama isn't happy, no one is happy. You can't think about MLC twenty-four hours a day, seven days a week. Yes, in the beginning, it consumes you, it's all you can think about, but you must break free, even if only for ten minutes a day. When your energy is depleted, it affects everything, including your attitude and all of your relationships. You can't be a good mother, wife, or friend if you don't take the time to do regular self-care.

It's important and a good idea to make a list of things that fill you up and bring joy to your life. Sometimes, just looking at this list can help you get unstuck and move forward with regular self-care. Having a list of activities and self-care practices to choose from adds variety to your life. They can be simple things that make you happy, such as buying yourself flowers every week. Early on during my husband's MLC, I started buying myself a dozen roses every week, and I continue to do so because it makes me happy. Your self-restoration activity could be taking a walk, going to Pilates or yoga, reading a book outside, having lunch with a friend, or having a nice long phone call with someone you love or a new friend who is in the same position as you. Massage is also important, even if you only do it once in a while. If your husband has left, you probably don't get touched regularly. We all know that physical touch is a valuable part of well-being and stress reduction, and massage is a great way to accomplish this.

Self-restoration also involves interacting with others. Whatever you do during this time, do not isolate yourself and sit at home. Force yourself to get out. Take a walk, enjoy nature, be around people. During the early years of the MLC, I forced myself to go out and have lunch, even by myself, once a week. I would take my laptop to Nordstrom Café, where it felt comfortable to be dining alone and working. I wrote a good chunk of my food prep book at Nordstrom. The wait staff got to know me, and we developed a nice connection.

When I moved out of state, I did the same thing. I started frequenting a restaurant once a week, took my laptop, and worked on my business. Again, connecting with people. Now when I walk in, they greet me and seat me at my favorite spot. It may seem scary going to a restaurant or a café by yourself, but take a good book or your laptop if you're uneasy about it. Connection is great self-care and key during this time. MLC can be a lonely time in your life, and these little connections mean a lot.

Here are some additional self-care ideas:

- Sit on your patio or deck.
- Take a nap.
- Write in your journal.
- Play Wordle or sudoku.
- Cook.
- Bake.
- Watch a good movie you love.
- Listen to a favorite podcast.
- Do Pilates or yoga.
- Walk.

- Meditate.
- Read.
- Get a manicure or pedicure or both.
- Have lunch with a good friend.
- Take yourself out for lunch.
- Work out.
- Join a sip and paint class.
- Go shopping, but only buy things for yourself.
- Browse the web.
- Organize an area in your house.
- Listen to your favorite music, but only if the lyrics make you happy.
- Make a favorite dish or a special meal.
- Call a good friend or family member.
- Take a walk in nature.
- Dance.
- Unplug from everything.
- Get or give yourself a facial.
- Get a massage.
- Water your plants.
- Work in the garden.
- Savor a good cup of tea.
- Go to a museum or art gallery.
- Put on lotion. I always hated putting on lotion until Cookie told me it was self-care, so now that's what I think about when I put it on. It is good self-care for your skin!
- Go on a local food tour.
- Go wine tasting with a good friend or friends.

- Take a trip by yourself. I usually go to my favorite beach for my birthday by myself, although sometimes I make it a girls' weekend.

Now it's your turn. Make a list and get started. Whatever you do is the right self-restoration for you, as long as it makes you feel good and nourished. One quick note to mention, while food and alcohol can be part of your self-care, they shouldn't be the only tools in your toolbox. It's easy to fall into using them to numb out instead of feeling your feelings. So, keep an eye on that.

The more you consistently invest in yourself, the more your brain starts to get the message: "We're safe, we've got this, we're moving forward. It's ok." This shift tells your brain you can move out of survival mode and back into your creative, thinking brain where you can start building a life you love, no matter what your husband is doing.

Welcome to Project You

I first heard this concept from my weight loss coach, Cookie Rosenblum, and it struck me hard... in the best way. Here's the truth: During your husband's MLC, you're not just surviving his personal storm, you're on your own journey to rediscover yourself.

My program, "Project You," consists of two parts. The first is to build yourself up to become the woman you want to be. Not the version of you who waits on your husband to change, but the one who becomes emotionally resilient, confident, and self-led, no matter what he does. Inside my Resilient Hearts Membership, I've created videos, reflection exercises, and activities to guide you through this process, step by step. Learn more at https://www.standingspouses.com/resilient-hearts

The second part is where you get to dream again, your dreams. You create a big, delicious, long-term goal, designed *by* you, *just* for you. This is a goal that lights you up, stretches you, and reminds you that your life still has purpose, meaning, and passion, with or without him. This goal isn't optional. It's essential.

If you want to rebuild your life—and if you want your husband to come back—yes, you must do both parts. Excuses like, "I don't have time" or "This won't work" are just fear in disguise. Trust me, you need this. Even if you have kids, especially during this season, you need to have a Project You. Think of it like being on a plane: You have to put your oxygen mask on first before you can help anyone else. And here's another reason: A heart on fire with passion is a highly attractive force in the universe. Let me give you an example.

> *Henry Ford said, "Whether you think you can or you think you can't, you're right." And he was. What you believe about yourself sets the tone for everything. If you lead with doubt, you stay stuck. But if you hold on to even a flicker of faith, you create momentum. Confidence isn't optional, it's the fuel that keeps you going.*

My own Project You started when I joined a mastermind for my blogging business. That one choice led to me writing a #1 book on Amazon, *The Power of Food Prep*, which led to creating a food prep membership. Having something big and meaningful to focus on during my husband's MLC was a godsend, especially since my children were older and out of the house. It occupied my days and nights. It gave me purpose, structure, and something to pour into while I navigated the chaos.

Other left behind spouses have done the same. My friend Jennifer became co-chair of her local Alzheimer's Association and started organizing annual fundraisers. Grace dove into Gam-Anon when her husband turned to gambling during his MLC. It's amazing what happens when you say yes to yourself.

My second big, almost impossible delicious goal in my Project You is no surprise. You are looking at part of it now. My original vision was to create Standing Spouses, a company with resources, a book, and a foundation with stipends for women to invest in education, training, childcare, or whatever self-care they need to rebuild. So far, it has turned into:

- Building the website standingspouses.com with my awesome virtual assistants, Kelly and Jill from Luminari Studios.
- Trademarking the term Standing Spouses.
- Getting certified in life coaching from Brooke Castillo.
- Creating Resilient Hearts, a highly specialized program just for you. A coaching program designed specifically to help you manage your thoughts, control your anxiety, learn the MLC basics, reconnect with your husband, alleviate the mental anguish and misery from the crisis, and create your best life, with a community of women just like you.
- Creating my Hope Beyond Heartbreak Course: Your Lifeline to Surviving Your Husband's Midlife Crisis (included in the Resilient Hearts Program).
- Developing and creating my "3 Minutes to Thriving Program" daily inspirations for left behind spouses.
- Becoming financially independent with a six-figure business (in the works).
- Officially hiring my best friends, Jennifer and Grace.
- Crafting the vision for creating a foundation in the near future.

Your circle should want you to win. Your circle should clap the loudest when you have good news. If they don't, get a new circle.
~ Unknown

I have turned my pain into passion, helping other women get through the hardest time of their lives. Now, it's your turn. Find your Project You. It doesn't have to be this big. You don't have to write a book or start a business. Figure out something you are passionate about, something that you can throw your whole self into that doesn't involve your husband. It could be going back to school, losing weight, getting in shape, being the best mom you can be, learning a new hobby, or helping others. You can solve so many of your own problems by helping others. Here's how to begin:

- Create your vision. Describe what you really want in great detail. What is something that will give you purpose and fill up your soul? What is your deepest desire? (Besides having your husband home.)

- Create a story web. Get a whiteboard, put what you think you want to do in the middle, and draw a circle around it. From there, draw lines out with things you want to do to create that vision. Try using a tool called Padlet that allows you to do all of this on the computer. I used it to design my Hope Beyond Heartbreak course.

- Gather ideas. Start collecting ideas and putting them on your Trello board.

Have faith and build your self-confidence in your Project You. When you think about your Project You, think about it in a positive light in order to stay in a creative state of mind. Negativity kills creativity, so avoid it, whether it is your negative thoughts or the negative comments from others. Find people who support you in your Project You. As you move forward, don't concern yourself with how your Project You will happen. The how will come. The more you start believing in your project, the more you will see the how begin to show up. The next steps will become clearer. When you think of your Project You, imagine that it has already happened, as if you have already succeeded. Don't be afraid of thinking too highly of yourself. You can do this. I know you can. I believe in you. It all starts with a dream.

What to Do Now

Start your Self-Restoration List by making a list of things that fill you up. Make a commitment to do at least three self-care things a day. They don't have to be big, but make them a priority. When you make time for them, even fifteen minutes a day, you'll see the benefits.

Next, shift your focus to Project You. Think of a huge, almost impossible goal for yourself. Write it down. Don't think about the how, just think about the what. It should really challenge you. Think from the point of view of your future self. "What would I be doing if I achieved this goal? How would I be living? How would I show up every day?" Imagine you meet me in person three years from now, what will you say to me: "Hi, I'm (your name) and I wrote this big impossible goal for myself, and I did it! I am now a __." Wouldn't that be great!

Along this journey, you have to surround yourself with the right people, those who are positive, who support your decision and lifestyle, and who resist sharing any negativity with you. Find your people and keep them close. Take action on your dreams and believe in yourself and your vision. Now, go create your own best life!

Key Takeaways

- Self-Restoration is nonnegotiable. You can't pour from a broken heart. Prioritizing your physical, emotional, and mental well-being is essential to surviving and thriving.
- Self-care is about restoration, not indulgence.
- Connection is part of the healing.

Chapter 11.

THE PAPER CLIFF—THE BIG D: A PIECE OF PAPER DOESN'T ERASE A CONNECTION

It's not the paper that defines the story, it's what you choose to believe about it.

~ Anonymous

Shifting from dreaming about your best life to facing the "D word" is a big, hard move, but you know we need to talk about it. Sometimes we try to avoid saying the word, "divorce," like not naming it will somehow keep it from crashing into our world. But avoiding the word doesn't make the fear go away. It just sits there, heavy, dark, and brooding.

As much as you want to ignore it, divorce looms in the distance like a storm on the horizon that you pray will pass, but deep down, you're afraid it's coming. And I know you're afraid of it because I was. Petrified, truly petrified. But here's the thing: Divorce, in the context of an MLC, is not what you think it is. Divorce is not the end of hope, it's not the end of your story, it's just a piece of paper. When you see it through the proper lens, it loses a lot of its power.

There's a reason I put this topic toward the end of this book. You need to understand what MLC is first. As you know now, MLC is not about the marriage, but the MLCer thinks it is. He thinks a divorce will make him feel better, that it will make him feel less guilty about everything he is doing to you and the family. But now that you know the truth about MLC, you are in the position to see divorce through the right lens.

My Story

One day, my husband texted: "I want to talk to you about something." I had a feeling it was coming, because he never wanted to talk about anything, so I was ready. My coach had done an excellent job of preparing me for this moment.

Later that day, I was at home making bread, had music playing, and I didn't hear him come in. He laughed when he saw me in the kitchen, singing and working on my bread. What he didn't know is that I had been preparing for this conversation for months. He sat at the kitchen counter, cleared his throat, looked up at the ceiling, over to the sink, then down at the hardwood floor. He was nervous. When he finally began, he couldn't even say the words, "I want a divorce." Instead, he said, "I d- d- don't think I- I- want to uh, well umm. I don't think I want to be married anymore." I could tell his heart wasn't in it by the way he stuttered the words, then spat them out of his mouth. He said something about this being the best thing for both of us and how much it was hurting him to say it.

I listened and then I told him, "If getting divorced will make you happy, then I can't deter you. It's not what I want for us and for our family, but I respect your decision. Ultimately, I want you to be happy."

With that, he just sat there and stared at me, speechless. He wasn't expecting my response to be about him and his happiness. I wasn't expecting to experience a flood of sympathy for him at that very moment. Through some tears, I asked if we could wait a few months before filing any paperwork. I had a lot on my plate. I was getting ready to move and my new book was launching. Adding this to my mental bucket would have been overwhelming for me.

He said, "It's just business." The comment was flat and matter of fact.

"Well, it's not just business, it's about my heart," I replied. In that moment, the flood of tears came, first from me, then, he put his hand on my knee, and he started to cry. I managed to propose a negotiation on the timing of the divorce until after my book came out and after the new house was built. He seemed both relieved that I didn't fight him and simultaneously excited that he had finally gotten it off his chest.

"Ok! Let's switch subjects," he blurted. Yes, he really said that. *Really?* I thought.

He then proceeded to talk about a number of random topics for another hour. I just sat there on the couch, looking down at the beige fibers on the cushion, trying to stay grounded in the moment, trying to appreciate the fact that he was still talking to me. I knew he just needed to talk, and honestly, I was relieved to have him there, rather than see him walk out after the initial shocking declaration of not wanting to be married. We talked about our kids and work. He then asked me about his parents. I told him they were devastated.

"About what?" He asked.

"About us being separated." I said quietly, stunned he didn't know. Seriously, he had no clue how this was affecting everyone else.

To top it all off, he had chosen to have the talk on our dating anniversary, the day we first started dating more than twenty-five years earlier. He didn't even realize the significance of that date before he decided to bring me that news. He later apologized profusely for being so unaware of his poor timing, but by then the damage had been done. Two days later, he asked if he could come over and smoke some hamburgers. I promise you; I couldn't make this stuff up.

My friend Jennifer sent me this text: "Ha! let me get this straight... two days ago, he comes over and tells you he doesn't want to be married anymore and then he comes over and y'all cook dinner together and he eats with you, and you hang out and have a good time? And he fixes things in the house for you?"

Crazy huh? This, my friend, is MLC. They don't know what they want, they just know they aren't happy with their life, and they think divorce is the answer to their internal pain.

Just as divorce won't solve his internal pain, it won't magically fix yours either.

Even though my husband made the decision to push for divorce, I want you to know that divorce isn't the end of the story, it's just a chapter, and often, a messy and confusing one at that. The bigger picture is that MLC isn't logical; it's about your husband's internal pain, not about you. His filing for divorce isn't about wanting his freedom. Instead, he is trying, and failing, to fix the brokenness inside himself, and divorce seems to him like a rational way to do that. When you accept this truth about my story and yours, you can hear about divorce during MLC without fear taking over. Even if divorce happens to you, you can still stand. You can still hope. You can still thrive. Divorce doesn't define you, your heart does.

For six months after my husband approached me about divorce I didn't hear anything more about it. In fact, he didn't file until almost a year later, and we didn't get divorced until a year after he filed. Most MLCers don't actually want to get divorced. For many, they resort to divorce because the affair partner is pushing for it. She might tell him, "You'll feel better if you just get a divorce. You need to move on so you can get some closure." Or, they push because they are at the end of their rope and don't know what else to try to make themselves feel better.

Think of divorce as just a piece of paper. Divorce doesn't erase your love. Sometimes, having that piece of paper is exactly what the MLCer needs in order to realize that the problem isn't external. Moving out didn't solve his problems, getting an affair partner didn't work, changing jobs didn't work, and (surprise) getting a divorce doesn't magically fix it either. He has to try everything he can think of before he figures out that the pain inside of him is the cause of all his problems. When he finally realizes he has to work on himself and find his happiness within, only then will healing take place. External solutions do not fix internal pain. This lesson relates to you too.

I have clients who tell me, "I can't stand living in limbo! I'm going to file for divorce before he does." Making this life-altering decision, not from a calm, grounded place, but out of fear and chaos—which is the same reason your husband wants to file for divorce—can be detrimental to your long-term happiness and to the potential restoration of your marriage. So, before you consider filing for divorce, I want you to pause and take a breath. Gain some clarity about your life, your dreams, and your relationship with yourself without reacting to the fear you might be feeling which, by the way, is normal. For now, ignore the pressure from well-meaning friends and family who might suggest that divorce is the best option for you. Instead, listen to your grounded, wise self, so that if you do choose to file, you do so from a place of strength, not survival or revenge.

Just as divorce won't solve *his* internal pain, it won't magically fix *yours* either. Lasting peace doesn't come from a legal document, it comes from managing your mind, healing your heart, and trusting yourself to make intentional choices with integrity. So, please read on if you are thinking about filing for divorce. My clients have said this has helped them continue to stand when they were ready to give up.

What to Consider Before You Decide to File for Divorce

If you decide you want to file for divorce, find a way to resolve your feelings about the marriage before you leave. If you blame the marriage for how you feel, you'll just find a new relationship—a rebound—to try to feel better. Remember, happiness is an inside job. You, not your partner, are the source of your happiness. You can be happy with anyone when you choose which thoughts to think. If you want to be happy with someone, find thoughts that make you happy to be with them.

Many MLC spouses think life will be better once they're divorced rather than living in limbo. However, unless you have clear reasons for filing, it's best to let your husband do it, because often it won't happen if it's up to him. Many people in your life will want you to give up and file for divorce because they think it will make you feel better. It won't make you feel better, and it won't bring you closure unless you have the thoughts to support it. Filing for divorce might make your friends and family feel better because they can see that you took action. And as tired as you are of MLC, they are even more impatient with it because they don't understand the nuances and realities of it. They are still reading from their old "manual" about what marriage should be, the one that tells them that if something unpleasant happens in a marriage, divorce is the next logical step. You are not bound by their beliefs.

We all want things to be black or white, this or that; but there is nothing in MLC that is black and white. Our survival brain wants us to make a choice because it doesn't like limbo. But surviving MLC requires you to use your prefrontal cortex, the thinking part of your brain. You have to look at the bigger picture. When you do, you will learn that you can get comfortable with the uncomfortable. Yes, you can actually learn to live in limbo if you have the correct thoughts about it. Thoughts like:

- "I can learn to live with the uncertainty because life is never certain anyway."
- "This midlife crisis is temporary."
- "I don't have to rush to make a decision."
- "Time is on my side."
- "Nothing has gone wrong; this is all part of the journey."
- "Staying gives me time to heal and grow, rather than make a rushed decision I might regret later."

So, before you decide to file for divorce, please ask yourself these questions:

- Why do I want to file?
- How will the situation be better if I file?
- How will it be worse?
- How will I feel after I file?
- What thoughts will I need to feel better after I file?
- How will I feel if I don't file?
- What will be different in my day-to-day activities?
- What thoughts will I need to live in limbo?
- What thoughts will I need to feel better about living in limbo?
- If I knew for certain my husband was coming home in six months, would I still choose to file? What about one year? What about two years?

Before you file for divorce, take the time to understand your motivations, manage your emotions, and make sure you're not just reacting to discomfort. Divorce won't give you the peace and closure you are looking for; your thoughts will. If you genuinely believe filing is the best path for you, do it from a place of clarity, not from frustration, fear, or anger. Don't file if you think it will make your husband come back to you faster. That is definitely not the case. You can't push him out of MLC. If you're filing to escape limbo, remember limbo is only painful if you think it is. You can stay right where you are, emotionally grounded, knowing this crisis is temporary. The more intentional you are with your thoughts, the more power you have over this experience, whether you file or not.

So, before you make any decisions, ask yourself: "Am I filing because I truly want to, or because I think it will make the pain stop?" If it's the latter, filing won't fix it, but managing your mind will.

Divorce Changes the Circumstances, Not the Connection

If you do get divorced, be prepared for a sudden change in your family and friends' attitude. Everyone generally thinks, "Oh good, she can move on now." It makes them feel better that you are no longer in limbo. In reality, divorce doesn't change anything between you and your husband.

Interestingly, divorce lowers his guard because he can hide behind the "divorced" title. Your husband never stops loving you, he just doesn't want to give you "false hope," a term commonly used by MLCers. He thinks that now that the divorce is finalized, it's ok to talk to you every day because he's not giving you false hope. He may start to communicate with you more. The truth is, you will always have a bond with each other, and he knows that. My husband even told me after he filed for divorce, "We will always have a bond. I will always love you." This too is part of the MLC playbook.

One of my friends said, "Before David came home, he would say, 'We'll always have a bond' and I would get so annoyed because he could never just say he loves me or whatever my egomaniac brain was thinking at the time. But now, I see he never stopped loving me, he just didn't want to give me the wrong idea when his life was in shambles." As it turned out, her husband did return home. Now that my husband and I are divorced, we still have a deep connection. I relied on him to help me through my mom's cancer and death. After the divorce, it seemed safe for him to be himself with me again and offer support. I never doubted that he was still there for me, but the constant communication and support proved it.

> Many times, after a divorce the MLCer will start communicating more frequently and seem happier, and then suddenly the connection takes a nosedive. This is because he often falls into a deep depression when he realizes getting divorced didn't work either. Be prepared for it.

If you do have to go through a divorce during your husband's MLC, remember that it is just a piece of paper. It doesn't erase the feelings, emotions, memories and love you've shared, or continue to share. So, if you find yourself walking through divorce—whether you initiate it or he does—just know that you are not powerless. This may be one of the hardest things you ever do, but you can do it with grace, strength, and intention. It won't be perfect, but it doesn't have to decimate you either. Here are a few practical things that helped me stay grounded during the divorce process.

Prepare yourself mentally before mediation. Take the day before your court date off from work and clear your calendar so you have plenty of time to get yourself ready. Mediation was an all-day Zoom call for me. I never saw his face, thank God, just my attorney and the mediator.

Write down statements that make you feel good. I wrote down these statements and had them near me as reminders:

- "There will come a time when your new, old heart is so strong that it will create things beyond anything you could plan with your mind."
- "Everything is working out for me in divine order."

- "God/The universe has my back."
- "Understand that this is still part of his MLC, this is what he needs right now."
- "Faith. Have faith in my attorney; that's why I hired her. She will do her best and it will be ok."
- "Have faith in the MLC process, meaning he will eventually come home."
- "Have faith in my successful business. I'm going to be ok. I will be financially independent. I will do this."

Make a list of everything you love about your husband. Keep this list handy on your desk or on notecards. Despite it all, the MLC is about his unhappiness, loss of purpose, and depression. Even though he convinced himself that he wanted the divorce, I had to review what I knew in my heart to be true. Here is the list I wrote:

> My husband loves me for me, he supports my business, he listens, he's kind, caring, would do anything for me, father of my boys, my rock, my hero, love of my life, sexy and intelligent, makes me laugh, educates me, puts me first, doesn't judge me, loves to travel, loves good food, likes quiet time like me, loves me despite my faults, is tender, caring, loves me whole.

I stayed strong through the entire divorce process. Only after it was over did I cry. The entire experience was awful for both of us. My husband was very generous, and I am very grateful for that. Neither of us felt better afterward, but we survived.

What Happens After the Divorce?

What you do next defines you. You get to decide who you become now. You get to choose how this shapes you. Will you let this break you or build you?

After the divorce was finalized, I continued with my unconditional love for him because that's who I am. It didn't end my love. Divorce didn't break me. That little piece of paper doesn't mean anything to me about our relationship. I know it's just a part of the process he had to go through. It didn't erase my commitment to becoming the best version of myself. I took all of these experiences and decided to think that my past has made me a stronger, nicer, kinder person. Whether or not he ever comes home, I am a better person for everything I went through. That is one of the silver linings of MLC for the left behind spouse. And then there's this: Even though I am divorced, I am still standing... full of hope, more anchored in love, and more certain than ever that beautiful things lie ahead for me.

Standing isn't about a legal status; it's about your heart and who you choose to be, no matter what life throws at you. You can be divorced and still stand for love. You can be divorced and still stand for your family. You can be divorced and still stand for yourself. That piece of paper can't take away the love you gave, the growth you gained, or the incredible woman you are becoming. So, if you find yourself divorced, breathe. Stand tall. Know that you are not broken, you are brave. And just like me, your story isn't over. Not even close. What will you make the experience mean?

This chapter of your life might look different than you planned, but it doesn't mean your entire book is finished. In fact, for many women, the more unexpected chapters are still ahead.

"You must give up the life you planned in order to have the life that is waiting for you."
~ Joseph Campbell.

What to Do Now

Above all, during this time, you want to be strategic. Don't engage in divorce talk with your husband. Don't bring it up. If he does, change the subject. Delay, delay, delay. Many men figure themselves out before it gets to that point. It took my husband and me two years to actually get a divorce after he said, "I don't want to be married anymore."

If your husband does file for divorce, refer to your attorney by their name (Susan), rather than as your attorney (my attorney). It may sound like a small detail, but it can soften the tone and feel less combative. In fact, using the attorney's name is a common recommendation in divorce mediation circles because it helps keep conversations more neutral and less triggering. In all communications, let the attorney handle the legal conversations. You hired them for a reason, so let the professional handle it. Don't get caught up in all of the muck of the divorce proceedings. That will ruin your relationship. Keep attorney talk to emails or other written communications for two reasons: 1) you have evidence of what was said, and 2) it allows you time to formulate an appropriate response and not say something unintentional in the moment or something that could be misinterpreted.

Prepare yourself before mediation or court appearances. Also, enter those environments with a loving heart. Remember what you have learned in this book: This MLC is an expression of your husband working through his internal struggles. The divorce is just part of the playbook.

If you are the one filing, be sure you ask yourself the questions in this chapter. Make sure it's not the external solution to your problem of living in limbo. As you become a better version of yourself, that feeling of being in limbo will pass and you will find reasons to continue focusing on your own happiness apart from your husband.

Thoughts are powerful. You get to decide what you want your past to mean. Will you take all these experiences and believe your past has made you a stronger person or will you decide to play the victim? It's all up to you. Your thoughts determine how you feel. What will you do? What will you make this mean?

Key Takeaways

- Divorce may just be a step/stage he has to go through to figure himself out. Try not to freak out about it. It's just a piece of paper, it doesn't mean all the love is gone.
- If you do get divorced, continue to be kind and loving.
- If you decide to file, make sure you have the right thoughts to back it up.
- You will be ok.

Chapter 12.

THE NEXT SUMMIT: RETURNING HOME AND THE NEW MARRIAGE

Sometimes, the greatest love stories are the ones rewritten after the fall.

~ Anonymous

Divorce didn't break me, and it doesn't have to break you either. Standing isn't about whether you're married or divorced, it's about keeping your heart open to love, hope, and healing... no matter what has happened. It's about who you decide to be when life doesn't go the way you planned. So, let's talk about something beautiful that isn't talked about enough.

Many times, they come home... even after the papers are signed and reconciliation looks impossible. You've been doing the work. You've been choosing yourself. You've been building a life you can be proud of, with or without him. Now, you might be wondering, "What if he actually comes back?"

Many husbands do come back, and most times, it's not like a big dramatic scene from a movie. It's more like he just quietly slides back in. At the time of this writing, my husband is not home yet, so obviously I can't write this from personal experience. However, my numerous friends and clients who have been through this, share one thing over and over: When you've remained kind, caring and supportive, and your husband feels that the door is still open, it makes it easier for him to slide back in. It's almost like he never left. I see traces of this when my husband comes to visit. It feels like old times.

One year around Christmas, he came to visit our son. My mom, who was still alive, was there for a month. Honestly, I think he wanted to visit everyone. He practically spent the whole weekend at our house. I remember it well. Mom sat at the kitchen table, I was in the kitchen making cookies to give to the neighbors, and my husband and son were at the counter where I was, talking about shooting targets, cleaning guns, and joining in our conversation. Christmas music played in the background, and I thought, *This feels like a normal holiday weekend.* Another time during that visit, he was lying on the couch, I was near his feet, my mom sat on the other couch, and we watched several episodes of *Julia*, at my mom's request because she loved that series so much. Later, we talked about our favorite movies, and he recommended some my mom would like. We probably spent two hours like that, just everyone sitting around, talking, and enjoying spending time together.

Several months after we were divorced, we all got together for my mom's celebration of life. He came for the weekend, bought my dad a grill, and helped me cook and serve all the food. Everyone in the family was confused because he acted like himself and even called me "Hon." They wondered if we were actually divorced because it felt like old times. These examples and more help me see how sliding back in and eventually coming home happens for many MLC couples.

Treat the Relationship as New

Oftentimes, when the MLCer finally returns home, he doesn't remember all the horrible things he did or said, and that's probably for the best. He may feel as though he doesn't deserve you. He probably will still be angry, not at you, but with himself. Or he could even be in awe of you because of the personal growth you exhibit, the way you've kept the household and your life together, the fact that you've kept your career or business going during this time, or because of new hobbies and interests you've developed. If this happens, receive his newfound respect and amazement of you. You deserve it! But don't have any expectations. This is key.

When your husband returns home, you must think of it as a brand-new marriage because it is. You have both transformed into new people. Take all of the lessons and knowledge you have learned about creating your own happiness and focus on creating a new life together. Don't dwell on the past, remind him of the things he said or did during the MLC, or bring up the affair partner. This won't help your new relationship. When he returns home, he's still broken, still confused, and still angry, mostly at himself. Don't beat him when he is down. Instead, continue to be kind and empathetic. Just take it slow. Be gentle. Be his friend.

Focus on all of the things you have learned. You know how to create your own happiness now. As he settles into being home, he will see how you have grown, and you know how to make yourself happy without him. Keep up the new self-care skills you learned when he was away. Meet your friends, spend time with them. Don't complain to him; complain to your friends if you need to. Give him lots of alone time. Let him be who he is. Don't expect apologies and don't try to bring up relationship talk, just let it all unfold naturally. Give him time and space to fit in again, to trust again. Just keep loving him unconditionally, and eventually, one day this will all be behind you. Keep up your gratitude journal, and keep focusing on the now and all the things you are thankful for. Be grateful for his return home, but don't get stuck on the why.

Women sometimes get hung up on what brings their husband home. This often gets in the way of the long-term goal. You have to remember your long-term goal: You want him home, and it doesn't matter why he comes home. He's probably figured out that life isn't better out there. He won't tell you that. He just wants to be home and spend time with his family because that feels good. He misses the family connection. One of my friends said, "I had to get over the fact that he wasn't coming home because he chose me. I knew that, but it still hurt. I had to deal with that, and it wasn't easy. I finally had to let go of that fact at some point. He still doesn't say he loves me, but he definitely shows me that he loves me with his actions, and that's what I have to focus on and be grateful for."

Stories from Standing Spouses Whose Husbands Have Returned

I asked my friends whose husbands have returned home to read my coming home section and add to it.

Grace

"I don't have regrets about standing. It was the right thing for me to do. Fears, yes, I have tons of those, but after going through everything, I can handle pretty much anything. And if it doesn't work out in the end, I can say I gave it my absolute all. Nobody can fault me or take that away from me. I did the best for my family.

I remember in the summer of 2023, there was a shift. He spent more time with us. Each time was longer than the last. Did he disappear? Did he say he would be back, but didn't come back when he said he would? Yes. But I didn't dwell on that and just kept it light and welcoming. I knew he was battling demons outside of us. The family was his safe space, and I knew that. Gradually, his perspective changed the more time he spent with us. Then, one day, he just stuck around and never left. There was no real conversation about, 'Oh, I'm staying now,' or 'I'm returning home.' Nor did I ask questions about whether he was staying for good. I just let us be and eventually let him lead with telling me.

In the beginning, he would be really careful about his wording. He would say, 'Let's see how it goes.' I assume he was trying not to set expectations too high because he knew what a mess he was mentally. I never pushed. Fast forward to now, at almost a year later, he tells me how grateful he is to have a fresh start with our family and that we're his number one priority now.

The hardest part when he is home is keeping my composure. You see glimpses of their old self, and you automatically want to fall back to how you communicated before. That would be a mistake because how you communicated before, I believe, played a role in this MLC. So, maintaining everything you've learned during this MLC when they are home is the ultimate test. I would also say keeping expectations low also helped me not jump the gun. Being more present and just accepting it's a process and this is just where we are.

But now, I see that he's turning around. He's spending more time with his children than he's ever spent. He acknowledges he has work to do on himself mentally and emotionally. It's no fairy tale, but I remember early on in the MLC all I wanted was to have my family together and happy. And by that definition we have that. There are moments of hair pulling, of course, but remembering where I was before helps me stay grateful for today, even when he is a jerk. And I know he feels the same way. It's like this unspoken thing where you've been to battle with someone and now there's a deeper bond because of the shared experience, even if it was him that set off the bomb."

Jennifer

"My experience has been that there was no fanfare, no declaration of love, no real apologies (when he came home). Mine agreed to work on us reluctantly and with little hope. There were still very few relationship discussions, I continued to focus on my personal growth and positive connection, tried to have no expectations (although, who doesn't). Mine had anger, lots of it toward me, but it took him almost two more years before he would even open up about it. Not long afterward, I ordered several fun couples books and asked him if he would consider reading one and following the instructions and he said he would look at them. He never did. I asked him to consider a game night with no TV, and his answer was, 'That sounds like too much of a commitment.' I started laughing. How ludicrous! Four kids, two businesses, and two houses; all these things together, but one night a week playing games was too much. He started laughing too.

We never did the game night. We never formally worked on our relationship. It had to be organic and non-structured. After he's been home for a while, I can say about 80 percent of our time together is positive, friendly, supportive, and good. If you look at our relationship and described it to someone else, they would say, 'Wow!' We are kind to each other, travel together, see friends, have the grown kids over often, and do nice things for each other regularly. Slowly but surely, he is somehow slogging through his issues and I'm here, trying to be a safe place, trying not to take things personally and trying to focus on my own path."

Jennifer's husband never technically moved out. He just busied himself with out-of-town work for over a year during the main part of the crisis and would come home occasionally on the weekends. Now, he spends much more time at home. She has been my friend from early on in my journey so I have really seen the progress in her husband, sometimes more than she can as I am an outsider looking in. At the time of this writing, they are on a family holiday cruise together. She just texted me that he bought her a necklace and was so excited to show it to her. She said, "I remember a trip in 2021 when I sat down in Disney Springs and bawled, and some random lady came to comfort me and pray. What a huge difference!" She went on to say, "I remember how horrible he was in the early days and how much he has changed. I think the thing to know is that MLCers don't just come home fixed and happy. There is still a lot of work to do together. It all takes time."

During the MLC you eventually learn that you can't control his behavior and that is a good thing. He is separate from you. So much of your identity in marriage before the MLC is caught up in "we" and our identities get lost. We don't have to like the same things. We can take care of our own self-care needs. We can be individual people, and that's what makes it a beautiful marriage. When you let him be him and you be you, you'll find two individual people who each create their own happiness first and then come together to create shared happiness.

"It's more than ok to hope."

If your husband isn't home yet just know it's more than ok to hope. You have permission to hope, despite what your friends, your family, your in-laws, heck even what your husband thinks. Hope is not a bad thing.

Plenty of husbands have said they are never coming home and they eventually return, even after they divorce. I know of seven couples in my small personal world who remarried each other after divorce. This is what gives me hope. While he may mean what he says at the time—that he doesn't want to be with you—eventually his mind clears. The fog lifts and he figures out what he truly wants. You can hold space for him while creating your best life and still hope that he returns to the marriage... and still know that if he doesn't, you'll be ok.

Final Thoughts

I wish you strength and peace on this journey you never asked for. I know taking that first step feels impossible, but you will take it, because life keeps moving forward. Life is always changing, and when you learn to see your circumstances as neutral (yes, even your husband's MLC), you open the door to creating new thoughts, new emotions, new actions, and ultimately, a stronger, better version of yourself.

There are silver linings, even in this. They're not always easy to see, but when you shift your perspective, they reveal themselves. I've found plenty, and here are my top three:

1. Family and good friends are everything.
2. Appreciate the now; don't stress about the future. Because I learned to stay present, I was fully there for my mom in the last year of her life. The unexpected silver lining of her passing? A deep, new bond with my dad.
3. I've got my own back. I've learned how to create my own happiness, no matter the circumstances. I know I'll be ok, come what may.

I don't know how my ending will turn out. But even if I find someone new, I know the lessons I have learned will help me in my next relationship. My hope, of course, is that my husband will return home and then I will write another book called *When He Comes Home: Life After Midlife Crisis*. But if that doesn't happen, I will be ok, more than ok. I know that now.

You can use your story of being a left behind spouse as an excuse for why you can't move forward, or you can use your story as the reason you create your best life. Post-traumatic growth is using your pain as fuel for your purpose and helping others. Although you can't change the fact that your husband's MLC happened, you don't have to be the victim in all of this. It doesn't have to define you. You are bigger than your circumstances. You can take what you've learned and create an amazing life, because of and despite all of this. You are not powerless, even though it might feel like your entire life has flipped upside down without your permission.

The world will tempt you to blame him, the affair partner, and the crisis. All of this keeps you stuck in pain that becomes a continuous loop. I've seen it with so many women who are bitter, even ten years later. Please don't let that happen to you. That bitterness only hurts you. The real power, the real healing begins when you stop reacting from your circumstances and start taking your power back. This doesn't mean that you caused his crisis or that what he's doing is ok. It means you get to decide how you will respond. You don't have to stay frozen in anger, resentment, and heartbreak. You are in charge of your life. Taking responsibility for your thoughts, your emotions, and your actions actually frees you. It unlocks growth, strength, and a version of you that's calm, clear, and unshakable, whether he comes home or not.

When you choose not to blame, when you stop waiting for him to change so you can heal, you start creating a life that feels good again. Your thoughts create your emotions. Your emotions fuel your actions, and your actions shape your future. If you stay stuck in blame, you stay stuck in the past. If you step into responsibility, you create a powerful future for yourself. You don't have to carry anger forever. You don't have to be bitter and broken. You are not powerless, no matter what your husband is doing. You don't build your future by waiting, you build it by choosing you.

So, what will your story be? Will you use the past against yourself, or will you take what you have learned and create an amazing new life? It's up to you. Make yourself the heroine in your own story.

And always remember: "Where there is love, there is always hope." ~ Hearts Blessing

ABOUT THE AUTHOR

*A*my Lawrence is a coach, author, and founder of Standing Spouses, where she helps women navigate the emotional chaos of their husband's MLC. Drawing from her own personal journey, extensive research, and work with women in crisis, Amy empowers them to stand strong, reclaim their identity, and create a life they love—whether their husband returns or not.

With a Master's in Special Education and an emphasis on behavior modifications, Amy blends science, mindset work, and practical tools to guide women with compassion and clarity. Her Resilient Hearts program equips wives with the strategies to manage their minds, build emotional resilience, strengthen communication, and develop the confidence to thrive during one of the most challenging seasons of their lives.

Before becoming a coach, Amy spent years as a special ed teacher, entrepreneur, and owner of a successful tea business and food blog. Her love for teaching and helping others has been a thread throughout her life—whether she was sharing gourmet cooking methods or now walking women through heartbreak and transformation.

A military brat born in Germany, Amy has lived across the US and Europe, and her travels have shaped her perspective on resilience, change, and growth. Today, she makes her home in Idaho where she continues to write, coach, and inspire women to believe in the possibility of healing and hope.

GRATITUDE AND ACKNOWLEDGMENTS

To my husband: This book was the hardest thing I've ever written, and a big part of that is because of you. Not in blame, but because I still care deeply. As much as this broke me, I know it broke you too. And I also know you never would have chosen this path on purpose. But without this journey, I might have missed some really important silver linings in my life, especially that final year and a half with my mom. The silver lining was the precious gift of enjoying the present. That time was a gift I'll always be grateful for.

To Jenn and Grace: There really are no words for you. You both showed up in the fire and kept me sane. I'll never forget that call in February and the way you both dropped everything and came to visit. You weren't just my lifelines during the hardest season of my life, you're also helping me build what came from it. Thank you for pouring your hearts, ideas, and energy into our Resilient Hearts Membership alongside me. Your belief in this work (and in me) makes it possible for more women to find their way out of the dark.

Gina: For being there in your quiet way. We have that bond. You know when I need your support. I don't have to say anything.

To my coaches who helped me through this:

Cookie Rosenblum, I'll never forget that day you opened my eyes to my thoughts.

Laurie McDermott, your videos saved my sanity. You helped me see there was life outside of MLC.

Brooke Castillo, your method changed everything for me. Your teachings and the practicum didn't just give me tools, they gave me a lifeline I could pass on to others. You helped me find purpose again, and a way to stand on my own two feet. I'll never stop being grateful.

To my coaches Jan Ditchfield and Liz Satterfield — You didn't let me give up on this book. Your words and encouragement have helped me more than you will ever know. Phrases like, "Tits up Amy!" and "F**k the mood, follow the plan," lightened my mood and kept me moving forward. I am forever grateful to you both.

Brianna Rossi, you have continued to support me no matter what I do. I am so grateful for your editing. Thank you from the bottom of my heart.

To my beta readers: Although I won't list your names, I thank you from the bottom of my heart for being the first ones to read my manuscript and for your suggestions and comments.

To my Resilient Hearts Members: Thank you all for trusting me with your hearts. I am so grateful to all of you.

To my parents: Mom and Dad, thank you for standing by me, even when the road did not make sense. Thanks for believing in me, even though you thought I was crazy.

My aunt and uncle: Thank you for those Friday nights. You'll never know how much they helped.

My mother-in-law and father-in-law: Your quiet support and daily presence meant the world to me. When everything felt upside down, you were there.

My sister-in-law: You were more than family; you were one of the people who helped me put my life back together, showing up after I moved, showing up on my birthday, taking trips with me, and reminding me what support looks like.

To my boys: You'll probably never fully understand why I wrote this book, and I hope you never have to. But I want you to know that everything I've done, especially the hard stuff, has been rooted in love, protection, and your future. You are both my heart. You are the reason I kept going, even when it felt impossible. More than anything, I wanted to set an example of what unconditional love looks like, even when life doesn't go as planned.

To my editor Anita: Thank you for taking a chance on me and thank you for giving me extra time because of my mom's death. I really needed it to sort through everything. I know I was quite a challenge, and I thank you for your patience and support. You are the best.

To my publishers Melanie Johnson and Jenn Foster: Words cannot express what a fantastic publishing team you are. You stuck with me through thick and thin. I am so grateful to you and for all of your support.

And to you, dear reader: You are not alone. There's still light up ahead. Let's walk this journey together.

AUTHOR'S NOTE

There have been many moments when I've thought, "Maybe writing this book isn't such a good idea." While it's meant to be a guide to help you navigate this horrible journey, putting my life—and my family's life—on display has never been the goal.

But I know how important it is for you (the reader) to feel understood and to know I've *really* been there. Just saying "I've been through it" doesn't build the kind of trust I want to have with you. It's a delicate balance—figuring out what to share so you can connect with my experience without sharing more than I'm comfortable with. Honestly, I don't even want my husband to revisit all of this.

I truly believe his MLC wasn't something he chose. He never wanted to hurt me or our family. This was him, lost and trying to find his way. And while this process shattered me, I believe it broke him too—maybe even more.

I hope he understands that I wrote this book not for attention, and certainly not to blame or shame him—but to help the women who are still in the thick of it. Because no one wants to talk about this. And yet, we—the ones left behind—are desperate for any nugget that might help us make sense of the madness.

My favorite resource, Hearts Blessing, never even shares her real name. And I understand why. I wrestled with whether I should attach my name to this too. But in the end, I knew it would reach more women if I did.

For five years, I saved quotes, articles, and resources on a little Trello board. Some I wasn't ready for yet, others I knew I'd need later. That board was my lifeline. And now, that has turned into your lifeline, this book.

I'm writing this with the utmost respect for my husband. I hope, if he ever reads it, he understands that. I've wanted to quit so many times—but then I remember *you*, the woman searching for hope. The one who needs to hear from someone who's just a little farther up the mountain, reaching back with a hand and a light.

I can't change what happened to me. And I can't change what's happening to you. But if this book helps you feel a little less alone in the dark, then every word was worth it.

ENDNOTES

1   Andrew G. Marshall, *I Love You But I'm Not In Love with You: Seven Steps to Saving Your Relationship*, (Bloomsbury Publishing, PLC, 2007).

2   Jessica Hall, "Gray divorce is most often initiated by women — even though it can crush their finances," MarketWatch, September 30, 2023, https://www.marketwatch.com/story/gray-divorce-is-most-often-initiated-by-women-even-though-it-can-crush-their-finances-4329540d

3   Saul McLeod, PhD, "What is Cognitive Dissonance?" Simply Psychology, June 20, 2025, https://www.simplypsychology.org/cognitive-dissonance.html

4   Brooke Castillo, host, "The Life Coach School." "Emotional Childhood vs. Emotional Adulthood," August 2, 2020, 10 min., 10 sec., https://www.youtube.com/watch?v=2nTEwrPiK4M

5   Sherri Gordon, "How to Recognize the Self-Serving Bias and What to Do," Health.com, September 14, 2024, https://www.health.com/self-serving-bias-8696388

6   Susan L. Brown, PhD, I-Fen Lin, PhD, "The Graying of Divorce: A Half Century of Change," The Journals of Gerontology, Series B, Volume 77, Issue 9, September 2022, pp. 1710-1720, https://academic.oup.com/psychsocgerontology/article/77/9/1710/6564346

7   Kara Oh, *Male Midlife Crisis: Why It Causes Men to Destroy Their Families, Finances and Even Commit Suicide, and What You Should Do*, (Avambre Press, 2014), p. 9.

8   Ibid, p. 7.

9   Hearts Blessing, "The Six Stages of a Mid-Life Crisis," https://thestagesandlessonsofmidlife.org/the-six-stages-of-a-mid-life-crisis/

10 Nicole Rosenberg, Klas Ihme, et al, "Alexithymia and automatic processing of facial emotions: behavioral and neural findings, BMC Neuroscience, May 29, 2020, https://bmcneurosci.biomedcentral.com/articles/10.1186/s12868-020-00572-6

11 Facial feedback hypothesis, Wikipedia, https://en.wikipedia.org/wiki/Facial_feedback_hypothesis

12 Kara Oh, *Male Midlife Crisis: Why It Causes Men to Destroy Their Families, Finances and Even Commit Suicide, and What You Should Do*, (Avambre Press, 2014), p. 57.

13 Dr. Bob Nguyen, *Midlife Crisis; Adapt, Evolve, Survive*, (Bob Nguyen, 2023), p. 55.

14 Bob Nguyen, M.D., Midlife Crisis; Adapt, Evolve, Survive, (Bob Nguyen, 2023), Ibid, p. 7.

15 Kara Oh, *Male Midlife Crisis: Why It Causes Men To Destroy Their Families, Finances and Even Commit Suicide, and What You Should Do About It*, (Avambre Press, Santa Barbara, CA, 2014), p. 53.

16 Brian D'Onofrio and Robert Emery, "Parental divorce or separation and children's mental health," World Psychiatry, first published January 2, 2019, (John Wiley & Sons, Inc.) https://onlinelibrary.wiley.com/doi/10.1002/wps.20590

17 Holly Uphold-Carrier and Rebecca Utz, "Parental Divorce Among Young and Adult Children: A Long-Term Quantitative Analysis of Mental Health and Family Solidarity," Journal of Divorce & Remarriage, 53 (2012): 4, 247-266, http://dx.doi.org /10.1080/10502556.2012.663272

18 Judith S. Wallerstein, *The Unexpected Legacy of Divorce: A 25-Year Landmark Study,* (Grand Central Publishing, 2001).

19 D. Kathy Nickerson, "4 Lies You Should Not Believe About Affairs," Facebook, November 25, 2024, https://www.facebook. com/share/v/171SbyiBw3/

20 Kara Oh, *Male Midlife Crisis: Why It Causes Men to Destroy Their Families, Finances and Even Commit Suicide, and What You Should Do,* (Avambre Press, 2014), p. 33.

21 Hearts Blessing, "I. Am. The. Wife.," https://thestagesandlessonsofmidlife.org/i-am-the-wife/

22 "Affairs That Become Marriages: The 9 Defects," The CHADIE Foundation, January 20, 2023, https://medium.com/@chadie/ the-9-defects-of-affairs-that-become-marriages-69cb5eab06

23 Elizabeth Landers, Vicky Mainzer, *The Script: The 100% Absolute Predictable Things Men Do When They Cheat* (Balance, 2005).

24 BrainyQuotes, https://www.brainyquote.com/authors/wayne-dyer-quotes

25 Amy Lawrence, *The Power of Food Prep: Take the Stress Out of Meal Planning with the Gourmet Done Skinny Method* (Elite Online Publishing, 2022).

26 "The science of gratitude and how it can affect the brain," Calm, February 8,https://www.calm.com/blog/the-science-of-gratitude

27 Andrew Humington, *The Neuroscience of Gratitude: Why Self Help Has it All Wrong* (Humington, 2023).

28 Dr. Joe Dispenza, *Breaking the Habit of Being Yourself: How to Lose Your Mind and Create a New One,* (Hay House, 2013).

29 Andrew Humington, *The Neuroscience of Gratitude: Why Self Help Has it All Wrong* (Humington, 2023), p. 54.

30 "Bob Proctor on Gratitude," Proctor Gallagher Institute, June 23, 2014, https://www.youtube.com/watch?v=c42aNPT68-Q